Quilting Bold and Beautiful

Hawaiian-Style Quilt Designs

Meg Maeda

Quilting Bold and Beautiful
Landauer Publishing, www.landauerpub.com, is an imprint of
Fox Chapel Publishing Company, Inc.

Copyright © 2022 by Meg Maeda and Fox Chapel Publishing Company, Inc.,
903 Square Street, Mount Joy, PA 17552.

HAWAIAN MOCHI-FU NO KIRUTO DEZAIN
Meg Maeda
© 2021 Meg Maeda
© 2021 Graphic-sha Publishing Co., Ltd.
This book was first designed and published in Japan in 2021 by Graphic-sha
Publishing Co., Ltd. This English edition was published in 2022 by Fox Chapel
Publishing. English translation rights arranged with Graphic-sha Publishing
Co., Ltd. through Japan Uni Agency, Inc., Tokyo.

English Edition Project Team
Translator: Freire Disseny + Comunicació
Editor: Christa Oestreich
Designer: Mary Ann Kahn
Indexer: Jean Bissell
Japanese Edition Project Team
Creative cooperation: Junko Iida, Sachiko Ishizaka, Keiko Kunou, Mitsuko Gunji,
Mai Shibuya, Yoko Misaki, Tomoko Miyajima, Yoko Miyata, Chiemi Rikitake
Art direction: Meg Maeda
Book design: Meg Maeda
Photography: Satoshi Fukuda
Diagrams: Miyuki Oshima
Editor: Ayako Enaka (Graphic-sha Publishing Co., Ltd.)
Manufacture: Junko Takaya, Sayaka Yanuma
Foreign edition production and management: Takako Motoki (Graphic-sha
Publishing Co., Ltd.)

ISBN 978-1-63981-016-1

Library of Congress Control Number: 2022944231

We are always looking for talented authors. To submit an idea, please send a brief
inquiry to acquisitions@foxchapelpublishing.com.

Note to Professional Copy Services:
The publisher grants you permission to make up to six copies of any quilt patterns
in this book for any customer who purchased this book and states the copies are for
personal use.

Printed in China
25 24 23 22   2 4 6 8 10 9 7 5 3 1

Contents

Introduction

"How do you come up with your designs? Do they simply come to you in a moment of inspiration?"

I get asked questions like these all the time. For me, designs happen whenever I take pen and paper and try to come up with them. It must be the result of having worked as a designer for so many years. After all, this is my craft.

Whenever a new project begins, I make loads of rough sketches. For inspiration, I look at photographs I've taken or search through my memories. However, if my design is based on things I haven't ever seen, I will of course begin by researching that topic. For example, my whale project began with a trip to the Ogasawara Islands. I can't possibly make a design based on something I haven't seen. Even if I tried to, that quilt would never convey any emotions. Then from a bunch of rough sketches, I choose the elements that most express the image's motifs and translate them into minimalist lines, thus creating a design.

Once the design is ready, my next step is to choose fabrics. I am an ambitious person, so I always want to include the emotions I felt when looking at the motif I've chosen, how the lighting made me feel, the wind, the temperature on that day, etc. Based on those memories, I search for fabrics that will convey it all as much as possible. Color is a part of design, as is giving it individuality.

The motif's main traits—its dynamism, beauty, color scheme, and originality—are countless elements that are fused into one, and a new design is born. Then, it's time to create the tapestry. Once the pattern design and the fabrics fit well together, we can see if it will be a good product once it's finished. Finally, I simply put my mind to sewing. I thread the needle as if I were a painter with a canvas. Once the tapestry is completed, you can use the symbolic sections of the design to develop cushions, bags, pouches, and other small, quilted objects. This involves cutting the design into its desired sections. That's one of the fun parts of working on designs: knowing that you can give one single design a variety of uses.

These are the steps I take to create a quilt, but my goal always, as a designer, is to generate entirely new styles. Secondly, I try to use shapes that would be easy to make use of in a Japanese household. My quilter friends from the United States call my quilts "designer's quilts." I guess they can see how the many years of me being involved in graphic design projects have greatly aided me in my quilting work. One of my purposes as an artist is, of course, to create these works. But I think an equally important purpose of mine is to bring high-quality designs to as many people as I can.

—Meg Maeda

■ Monstera

A monstera is a plant whose large leaves are covered in many notches and holes. This motif is a lot of fun to work on since it allows you to be very bold with your trimmings without making the pattern look bad. This is because it's such an idiosyncratic design.

Instead of letting the entire leaf show, if we make a design that extends beyond the quilt size we're working in, we can help emphasize how big monstera plants actually are.

01 The Flowers That Bloom at Akaka Falls

This is a redesign of a quilt with the same title that I made fifteen years ago. The design, fabrics, and quilting techniques I have used are all different than last time.

The motif is more faithful to the real plant, and the fabric has a natural indigo dye. As for the quilting technique, I have focused on thread thickness and needle pitch. Monotone fabrics give this quilt an interplay between stillness and movement.

Size: 43¼" x 43¼" (110 x 110cm) How to make: page 64

02 Single Huge Leaf

I cropped a section of the monstera tapestry design and then enlarged it. This single leaf fills the whole frame, which allows us to really see how huge monstera are. This colorful, framed quilt would look great hung on a wall or placed against it on the floor.

Size: 22" x 13⅜" (56 x 34cm) How to make: page 65

03 Monstera Cushions

I cropped two 17¾" (45cm) squares from the previous design and made cushions with them. The charm of this plant's leaves is that, even when cropped at such a detailed level, they're instantly recognizable as monstera. Inverting the colors in each cushion emphasizes that they're two different designs.

Size: 17¾ x 17¾" (45 x 45cm). How to make: page 66

04 Geometric-Print Monstera Bag

When making designs that play with silhouettes, geometric patterns are a perfect combination. Using two solid colors is the coolest option. I'd recommend choosing striking color combinations, such as black and white or Saxe blue and brown.

Size: 9⅞" x 13¾" x 2⅜" (25 x 35 x 6cm). How to make: page 68.

Lilikoi

A few years ago in early summer, I visited the *lilikoi* (or passion fruit) farm on Hahajima, one of the Ogasawara Islands. The owner of this farm always sends me lilikoi when the season for this fruit begins, and that summer he was kind enough to let me see a lilikoi farm for the first time. I sketched the scenery, totally absorbed by it: countless trellises on which each stem spread into several vines, growing into fruits covered by thick foliage.

My design centers around these three characteristics of the lilikoi: its vigorously outstretched vines; its idiosyncratic, three-pronged leaf; and its sagging purple fruit.

05 The Purple Fruit of Ogasawara Island

This color scheme makes for a really striking composition: green, like the thick foliage and many vines that spread on the farm's trellises; purple, like the fruits that adorn all those leaves; blue, like the sky and sea. The pattern design and fabric colors made this quilt turn out exactly as I imagined it. Twisting, twining lilikoi.

Size: 63" x 43¼" (160 x 110cm). How to make: page 67.

The lilikoi fruit is packed with tiny seeds. I used a backstitch technique to make sure these were visible.

Rectangular Lilikoi Bag

This bag takes the longest vertical crop you can make from the Purple Fruit of Ogasawara Island tapestry and aligns it horizontally in a 1:2 ratio. The main motif uses the same fabric as the tapestry, but the background fabric has been replaced with a slightly casual print. Bags with no gusset really look much sharper. This bag on your shoulder is a stylish look.

Size: 9⅞" x 19⅔" (25 x 50cm). How to make: page 70.

Framed Lilikoi Quilt

If large designs feel hard to give a decorative use, try making a smaller, framed version of them. Despite it being shrunk, the elements of this design are still the same. Adding a frame gives the quilt a formal look.

Size: 27¾" x 17⅛" (70.5 x 43.5cm). How to make: page 72.

08 Threefold Lilikoi Case

This case uses the smallest possible crop of the lilikoi design but still keeps enough elements to be recognizable. Since this project is a small item you would carry around, I felt a bright color, like magenta, was best. This way it would vividly stand out inside your bag.

Size: 7⅞" x 4¾" (20 x 12cm). How to make: page 73.

Banana Leaves

Banana leaves are motifs used often in Japanese designs. When the wind blows, these huge leaves sway and their delicate veins tear. This produces an even more refreshing look. Their simple silhouette makes one imagine the warm breezes of southern countries.

09 Three Banana Leaf Panels

Folding screens were my inspiration to make three quilts from the same design. But by using panels, you get a fun sense of thickness and three-dimensionality. They can be hung on flat or curved walls. An all-new way of using quilts to make unique wall art.

Size of each panel: 21¼" x 15" (54 x 38cm). How to make: page 74.

10 Stitched Banana Leaf Tote Bag

A large tote bag embroidered with a backstitched design of banana leaves. The refreshing texture of the unbleached cotton-linen blend is combined with the bright red threads and leather strap.

Size: 13¾" x 15¾" x 7⅛" (35 x 40 x 18cm). How to make: page 75.

11   Stitched Banana Leaf Pouch

A flat pouch, the twin accessory to the tote bag. Its zipper is also red to maintain the color scheme. This time I only stitched the silhouette.

Size: 4½" x 7⅞" (11.5 x 20cm). How to make: page 76.

■ Ulu

Ulu (or breadfruit) is a beloved plant for Hawaiians, esteemed as a symbol for growth and abundance. Also, it's famously a common first motif people choose when starting to quilt. This design is one of the most familiar for quilters.

12 Under a Huge Breadfruit Tree

A friend of mine, Nick, has a huge breadfruit tree by his house on Hilo, an island of Hawaii. If you sit on the lone bench that's placed right under it, you can hear the tree breathing. Its thick branches grow freely while the breadfruit hang heavy, showing their tiny faces through the fan-like leaves. It's one of my favorite spots, one where even the cool air seems to acquire a greenish tint.

Size: 63" x 43¼" (160 x 110cm). How to make: page 77.

13 Small Breadfruit Tapestry

Here, I've cropped a section of the characteristic elements of the design: the branches, leaves, and fruits. The fact that this design doesn't fully fit into the approximately 20" (50cm) square helps to show how vigorous and energetic breadfruit trees are. Such a lively design needs a lively fabric. I chose to do the binding with batik fabric, a unique material because it is hand-dyed, which gives a very attractive result.

Size: 20⅞" x 20⅞" (53 x 53cm). How to make: page 78.

14 Breadfruit Cushions

Like the Breadfruit Tapestry, here I cropped sections I liked from the quilt pattern. Each cushion has a slightly different design, and the fabrics have been inverted for each. The color variation really does give them a different look.

Size: 17¾" x 17¾" (45 x 45cm). How to make: page 79.

Rainbow Shower Tree

Different shower trees have different flower colors, but the rainbow shower tree is a hybrid, meaning the colors of its flower petals are mixed. As the official city tree of Honolulu, it is often planted by roads and easy to spot, delighting people whenever it blossoms.

15 Big Shower Tree Tapestry

The key elements of this design: the small grape-like petals, so amazing and lovely; the leaves, which grow left and right in strangely tidy rows; and the sturdy trunk, which grows to truly massive sizes. Each flower has been individually quilted to let them stand out.

Size: 86¼" x 86¼" (219 x 219cm). How to make: page 80.

16 Flowery Shower Tree Tapestry

In this version that has been shrunk to 39⅜" (100cm), the orientation of the motifs has been flipped around. This way, it doesn't simply become a smaller version of the bigger design. It becomes its own quilt, with themes that are not outmatched by the larger tapestry.

Size: 39⅜" x 39⅜" (100 x 100cm). How to make: page 81.

17 & 18

Shower Tree Square Bag & Semicircular Pouch

I cropped a quarter of the Flowery Shower Tree Tapestry and used it, without any changes, to make a bag. Since the bag is square, too, I could use the entire crop as its design. For the pouch, which is smaller, I kept only the symbolic elements of the motif. This smaller design only includes the tip of the flowers and the leaves.

Bag size: 13¾" x 13¾" x 2¾" (35 x 35 x 7cm). How to make: page 82.
Pouch size: 6⅓" x 11¾" (16 x 30cm). How to make: page 84.

■ Lokelani

Lokelani is Hawaiian for "rose of heaven." Despite this rose being an introduced species, the name it was given truly shows how much it's loved by Hawaiians. This double-petaled, dark pink flower, which is especially aromatic, has been called both the Maui Rose as well as lokelani. It is the official flower for the island of Maui.

19 Garden of Blossoming Lokelani

As I strolled past a house on the island of Maui, pink enveloped my field of vision. Innumerable double-petaled roses. I can still recall their vivid colors and their indescribably sweet smell. I turned that powerful memory into this quilt, with its powerful color combination of pink and magenta.

Size: 63" x 43¼" (160 x 110cm).
How to make: page 85.

Lokelani **33**

20 Rose Blooming from the Frame

At some point, flat surfaces stopped satisfying me, so I began creating 3D flowers. This one pops out of the quilt, bringing a great presence to the rest of the 2D quilt. A quilted rose and a 3D rose. Stillness and movement contained in one small frame.

Size: 19⅔" x 11½" (50 x 29cm). How to make: page 86.

21 Semicircular Bag with Lokelani

I took the flower design from the Garden of Blossoming Lokelani pattern and turned it into a stained glass quilt bag. When doing appliqué, it's important that the thickness of the lines is never exactly the same. If the lines vary in size, it makes the motifs look lively. The combination of yellow and cool gray creates a refreshing look.

Size: 11¾" x 23⅔" (30 x 60cm). How to make: page 88.

22 Lokelani Sewing Case

Like with the Semicircular Bag, I made a stained glass quilt of a single flower to use for the exterior lid. The inside lid, body, and bottom sections are decorated with flower bud patterns. In quilting, if the design becomes unclear, you backstitch its outline with embroidery thread.

Size: 4⅜" x 6⅓" x 3⅛" (11 x 16 x 8cm). How to make: page 90.

■ Marine Life

Marine life, as a motif, is never missing from my quilts. It includes many fun design motifs, like whales, sea turtles, sand dollars, or sometimes even geckos. And of course, any creature I haven't seen with my own eyes I will not be able to make a design from. So whenever I take a trip for reference, I make sure I encounter the animal I am trying to meet.

23 Sperm Whale Swimming in a Glittering Sea

The Ogasawara Islands are the ideal place to see whales, and I actually met the sperm whale I wanted for this design. Unlike humpback whales, sperm whales have teeth and hunt giant squids, so they live at a depth of approximately 3,000 feet (1,000m) underwater. We searched for one by using underwater sound sensors, which cover a wide range of the ocean. Luckily, a sperm whale rose close to the surface and swam in the direction of the boat. It was a huge one. It had a huge body and small pectoral fins with tiny eyes very close to them that were staring at me. It looked at me! I doubt I'll have an experience like that again. After it swam away, the sea glittered with a blue tone that felt as if the rays of sun were covering every single part of it.

I depicted that sea and the sperm whale with a stained glass quilt. I applied white fabric to stitch the sky, adding a sense of balance with the sea.

Size: 41⅓" x 41⅓" (105 x 105cm). How to make: page 92.

24 Swimming Whale Bag

I also saw a humpback whale in Ogasawara in March. It's a month when they tend to rear their children, so the whales come to shallow waters near the island. This made it much, much easier to find one than it was to find a sperm whale. The humpback whale we saw was swimming so energetically that it reminded me of a yacht gliding across the water and splashing everything around it.

I used a semicircle shape for the bag, which brings the humpback whale design to life. Its tail design was too big to fit (after all, it's a massive animal), so I put it on the back of the bag. The humpback whale pattern, as well as the whirlpools and waves in the water, were all backstitched with a thick quilting thread.

Size: 11¾" x 23⅔" (30 x 60cm). How to make: page 94.

25　Snoozing Sperm Whales Bag

Sperm whales sleep in groups, positioned vertically. That's why this is a vertically shaped bag. The shape of each whale is almost too simple, which makes it hard to use as a motif. But if you place enough of them together as appliqués, it makes a fun design. A key feature here is the use of yellow for the handle, which is a striking complement to the other colors.

Size: 14¼" x 9½" x 2⅜" (36 x 24 x 6cm). How to make: page 96.

26　Exercising Sperm Whales Pouch

Sperm whales going for a short wander after lunch. They exercise to help with digestion. When I'm stitching their tiny eyes, I clearly remember the sperm whale that looked at me that day. I didn't add many quilt lines, opting instead for a plump finish. And of course, finished with a yellow zipper.

Size: 7⅞" x 11¾" (20 x 30cm). How to make: page 93.

27 Small Manta Ray Bag

In Hawaii, there are many spots where you can see manta rays. I'm a little bit scared of them, so I haven't tried swimming with them yet. The Polynesian manta ray has a green sea turtle design incorporated on its back. It's a dream of mine to one day swim alongside them.

Size: 11¾" x 11¾" (30 x 30cm). How to make: page 98.

28 Small Green Sea Turtle Bag

On the island of Hilo in Hawaii, there's a peaceful cove where green sea turtles nest. Some years ago, while I was taking photographs for my quilts, they swam right next to me all the while. I incorporated a bone hook design on its back.

Size: 11¾" x 11¾" (30 x 30cm). How to make: page 98.

On the back of both the manta ray and green sea turtle bags, I backstitched Polynesian designs of waves and sand dollars.

29 Sand Dollar Folded Pouch

I made a lot of small appliqué sand dollars, since I love how they look, and sewed them onto this base created from different patches arranged in color gradation. The sand dollar's tiny holes, which are popularly said to be filled with happiness, are made with reverse appliqués the size of a grain of rice.

Size: 5⅞" x 7⅞" (15 x 20cm). How to make: page 100.

30 Stitched Wave Tote

A turquoise backstitch over a blue Oxford cloth. It's a Polynesian design representing waves. The beige leather handle adds some mildness to the overall color scheme.

Size: 13¾" x 15¾" x 7⅛" (35 x 40 x 18cm). How to make: page 102.

31 Seahorse Pouch with L-Shaped Zipper

For this pouch, I had fun using printed fabrics. It's composed of various small scraps of material, without binding. I added an L-shaped zipper to make the pouch easy to open and close with one hand.

Size: 4" x 7⅞" (10 x 20cm). How to make: page 104.

32 Gecko Pouch with L-Shaped Zipper

In Japan, geckos are called yamari, and they're a beloved motif said to protect households. To avoid it looking too realistic, you can do an appliqué in bright colors. Also, polka-dot patterns are perfect for accessories, aren't they?

Size: 4" x 7⅞" (10 x 20cm). How to make: page 104.

33 Banana Leaf Pouch with L-Shaped Zipper

The design only depicts the shape of the banana leaves plus their central veins. This lime green appliqué over a yellow print offers a very banana-like look.

Size: 4" x 7⅞" (10 x 20cm). How to make: page 104.

Landscape

About 17 years ago, I started sewing Hawaii's amazing landscapes into quilts. The lovely Mauna Kea Beach is covered in blossoming flowers. On Bali Hai Beach in the island of Kauai, one can see the flowering plumeria glowing in the sunset. It was with my landscapes that I began developing my new 3D flower technique. This added something novel, which wasn't present in Hawaiian quilts.

34 Kaimana Hila

Kaimana Hila is the Hawaiian name for Diamond Head. This mountain is part of the landscape on the island of Oahu. This composition shows the view you get from Waikiki Beach, which is a place everyone knows.

I decorated it with palm trees and 3D bougainvilleas. The three small spheres within each bougainvillea are actually the flowers. In this case, I chose to represent them with beads.

Size: 15¾" x 15¾" (40 x 40cm). How to make: page 105.

35 Bali Ha'i Sunset

Makana Peak, on the northern shore of Kauai, was used to depict the legendary paradise Bali Ha'i in the Hollywood movie South Pacific. Several years ago, I made a reservation for a terrace seat at a Princeville hotel just so I could see the stunning "Bali Ha'i" sunset.

The black of the palm tree silhouettes and the black border create a strong contrast with the colors of the sky. The plumeria, which filled the twilight with their sweet aroma, made a big impression on me.

Size: 16½" x 20½" (42 x 52cm). How to make: page 106.

36 Moonlight Manta

Every night, in the tiny bay of Keauhou on the island of Hawaii, manta rays come to swim. Seeing their fluttering fins rise to the surface, all white because of the moonlight, was so magical that seeing them in that spot became what I would most look forward to. The gradation of colors of the moonlit sea was created with appliqué. Deep red laceleaf becomes a prominent element.

Size: 17" x 17" (43 x 43cm). How to make: page 108.

Quilt Lesson

Even though designing is hard, cropping a design from an already existing pattern is easy. You can combine different parts or just partially crop a pattern.

Now I will try to teach you how to develop a design as well as provide the traditional instructions for how to quilt.

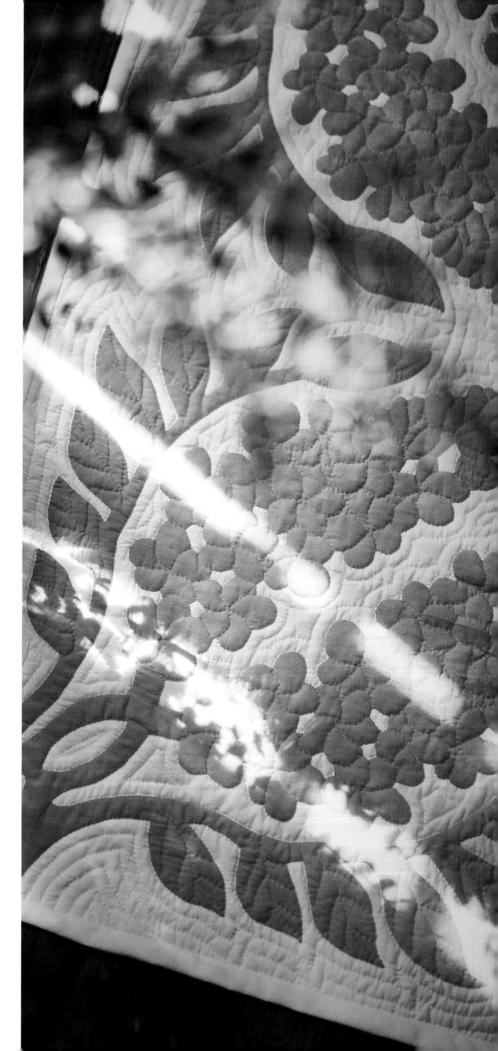

How to Manufacture Designs

I will now explain how to develop designs into small accessories. Create accessories with your favorite designs and feel free to adapt them to your own taste.

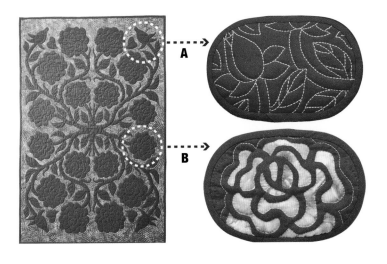

Example 1—Lokelani

A

The interior lid and body are a stitched quilt since I wanted them to bring balance to the exterior lid. Since I was stitching a design onto a very small area, a composition of delicate buds and leaves was a better choice than big, blooming flowers.

B

The sewing case's exterior lid needed an impactful design; in this case, I chose a large flower. It's a design that allows you to make use of its quilt lines just as they are, so I used the stained glass quilt method. This allowed me to get the same pattern to look like a completely different design.

Example 2—Lilikoi

C

I cropped the section of my tapestry that had the most variety of forms. Its width and length were proportionally different, so when applying it to the bag's actual size, I made a few minor adjustments to make it fit better overall, such as modifying the spaces between shapes or the curvatures of the leaves. Furthermore, since its size is different from the quilt's, you can simplify some of the subtle parts that would be hard to sew, such as the curls of the vines, and so on.

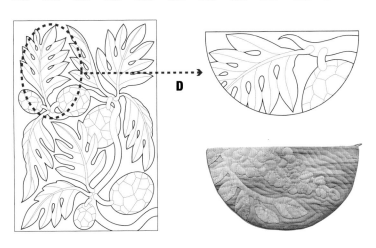

Example 3—Application: Applying different designs to an accessory

D

A breadfruit design could be applied in the same way as the Shower Tree Semicircular Pouch from page 84. I cropped a section from the tapestry that had a good balance between leaves and fruits. Then, I reversed it while making sure it fit. Make sure to crop the design so that all motifs can be clearly grasped. This way, the breadfruit's vitality and dynamism is maintained in the image.

How to Quilt

I will explain how to make these Hawaiian quilts from start to finish, starting with copying the motifs and ending with the binding. Appliqué is fundamental to some of these projects, but I will also explain how to do reverse appliqué. This involves carving the top fabric (the base fabric) so that the bottom fabric (the motif fabric) can then be seen. I will also explain how to make three-dimensional flowers.

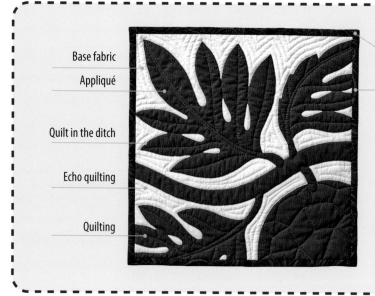

Base fabric

Appliqué

Quilt in the ditch

Echo quilting

Quilting

Border

Bias tape Double binding

Instructions

1) Copy the sketch (the motifs) onto the appliqué fabric.

2) Cut the appliqué fabric and attach the appliqué onto the base fabric to create a top.

3) Pile the top, created in step 2, over the backing and the cotton batting. Tack all three pieces and begin quilting.

4) Bind the edges and you're done.

Note: I have kept the stitches big to make the images easier to discern, and used threads of striking colors, like red, to make them more visible. When sewing, however, try to make the stitches small and keep the thread color as close to the fabric's color as you can.

1. Copy the motifs onto the fabric

1 Prepare your sketch, your appliqué fabric, and your base fabric. Iron them and smooth out any wrinkles.

2 Layer the appliqué fabric, a sheet of tracing paper, the sketch, and cellophane in that order. Make sure the sketch and the fabric are aligned. Use a tracer to outline the sketch lines. Outline the quilting lines on the inside of the sketch.

3 While copying the sketch, layer the appliqué fabric and the base fabric, making sure they're aligned, and keep them in place with a marking pin.

4 Tack all around the sketch. Sew at intervals of around ⅜" (1cm) with thread that is placed more or less ⅜" (1cm) in from the sketch line. Once you've tacked all of it, you can start doing the appliqué.

2. Doing appliqué: Basic slip stitch

1 Add about ⅛" (3mm) of seam allowance and then cut the outer side of the sketch. Don't cut it all in one go. Make a small cut and then sew it, repeating these steps again and again.

2 Keep the edge of the line pressed down with your thumb and fold the seam allowance inside with the tip of the needle. We will use an appliqué needle.

3 Make the needle exit from the appliqué fabric's pleat, and insert it directly into the base fabric underneath. Then, make the needle exit again from the appliqué fabric's pleat a scant ⅛" (2mm) from where it is now. Blindstitch, repeating these steps.

4 The seam will line up at regular intervals, as shown in the image.

Concave curves

1 As shown in the image, make cuts aligned with the curve into the seam allowance. If the curve is in the direction of the bias, you don't need to make many cuts.

2 Blindstitch until you're about ¾" (2cm) in front of the curve, then stop the needle there. Insert the needle into the seam allowance on the other side of the curve, and fold said allowance.

3 Point the needle away from you and rotate it horizontally to fold the seam allowance. Turn the needle around as if drawing a smooth curved shape.

4 Continue doing this until you've connected it all up to the pleat that you're blindstitching. If you rotate the needle around, the seam allowance will fold naturally.

5 Blindstitch until the curved section. The curved section has cuts made into it, so you will have to blindstitch by ejecting the needle from the inner side, more than you did during the straight sections.

6 Make sure you are blindstitching as if you were doing a very fine whip stitching at a scant ⅛" (1mm) intervals.

7 Once you've passed the curve, you can go back to blindstitching at ¾" (2cm) intervals.

V-shaped indentations

1 Blindstitch from the bottom side of the V-shape to ¾" or 1⅛" (2 or 3cm) away in your direction, and stop the needle there. Make a cut on the right side of the V-shape. This task is easier if you use small scissors with a curved tip.

2 Insert the needle into the cut on the bottom of the V-shape, and begin folding the seam allowance.

3 Continue this way until you've connected with the pleat you're blindstitching. Sew a slip stitch until you're about one needle's distance away from the bottom of the cut in your direction.

4 Make the needle exit from the bottom. If there is no seam allowance (the pleat) on the bottom, then fold just a bit of the inner side of the curve.

5 Now fold the next section of seam allowance toward the bottom with the tip of the needle.

6 From that position, insert the needle into the bottom and start blindstitching.

7 Blindstitch two needles' distance at the bottom of the curve. Make the needle exit at the next section and blindstitch some more.

8 The stitch will look like this. Whenever the V-shape becomes difficult, it's no problem to just blindstitch the curve.

Pointed sections

1 We will delicately blindstitch until reaching ⅛" (3mm) before the pointed corner. Thanks to blindstitching delicately, we can prevent the tip of our next folded seam allowance from showing through.

2 Take the needle out through the corner and keep it there for a while.

3 To avoid the folded seam allowance from poking through the next section, cut all the remaining seam allowance.

4 Fold the tip's seam allowance at a perpendicular angle to the needle.

5 Insert the needle into the next section, and fold its seam allowance. Keep it pressed with your thumb to create a sharp, angled point.

6 Insert the needle into the base fabric underneath and blindstitch, poking it through out of the next section. Now blindstitch around the pointed corner with a lot of care.

7 Blindstitch the next section in the exact same way. Finally, you've sewn a beautiful sharp corner!

3. Tacking: Starting to quilt

1 After finishing all the appliqués, the top is complete. Now we must draw the final lines we'll use to make an echo quilting evenly spaced around the appliqué.

2 Draw the echo quilting lines ⅜" (1cm) away from the appliqué around the entire original sketch, keeping balance with it. It isn't a problem if tighter sections are drawn at ¼" (8mm). Plan for the final lines to shrink once you sew them, so it's better to add a little extra all around.

3 Sandwich the finished top over the backing and the cotton batting. Align it well and smooth it with your hands.

4 Stabilize all important positions with marking pins. Start tacking. Radiate from the center in a cross shape, then do diagonal lines, and finally divide those diagonal sections into thirds.

5 Add some support cloth to make it easier to quilt right up to the edge. Fold the support cloth in half, layer it over the outer edge of the final lines, and use a double strand of tacking thread to sew even more finely than your tack was sewn.

6 Now that you've attached support cloth around your border, this will make it big enough for the hoop to be inserted right up to the edge.

7 Place the hoop's inner border under the quilt and insert the outer border from above. Push the quilt up from behind in equal measures to loosen it up a bit. If you loosen it, it's easier to press the needle through.

8 Insert the needle from any spot that's ⅜" (1cm) away from the quilting line, pierce only through the top fabric, and make the needle exit through the line. Threads used for this are traditionally between #40 and #50, but this time I've used a slightly thicker thread, between #40 and #30.

9 Pull out the thread, make a thread knot, and drag it back inside the fabric. This way, the thread knot won't be seen from the surface, which makes it prettier.

10 Put a thimble on your middle finger. Use the ball of your finger to push the needle from the inside toward you, stitching all three layers of fabrics at the same time.

11 Insert the hand that isn't holding the needle into the reverse side of the quilt (the reverse side of the fabric), and use those fingertips to keep track of where the needle is, making sure it pierces all three layers. Once you've made three or four stitches, remove the needle.

12 Quilting a scant ⅛" (1mm) away from the edge of the appliqué is called in-the-ditch quilting. It makes the motifs stand out even more, so I always use it. It is done with the same method as regular quilting.

4. Binding: The finishing touches

1 Now that you've finished quilting, you can remove the tacking.

2 Redraw the quilt marks, following the actual size of the quilt, and cut through them. Using a rotary cutter to snip those straight lines gives a prettier finish.

3 Create some bias tape. Place your chosen fabric at a 45-degree angle and make its edges touch in the center. By folding it this way, you will be able to cut a very long section of bias.

4 You won't use the triangular folds on either side. Use the bias tape to create two-fold double binding; cut at a width of 3 ¾" (9.5cm). You can calculate this width by multiplying the width of the binding (in this case 1" [5mm]) by 6. Note: for metric, add 5mm to round it up to a convenient number.

5 Cut four pieces, all adapted to the length of the quilt's edges. Make sure the diagonal lines for each side are facing in the same direction, and connect them with bias tape.

6 Add marks for ¼" to ⅜" (7 to 10mm) of seam allowance, and stick marking pins in those marks. The key is to slide the edges to make them align. If you don't slide them this way, you would encounter differences in alignment when spreading out the bias tape, so you wouldn't get a straight section of bias.

7 Sew over the marks, fold the seam allowance to one side, and spread the bias. Any extra seam allowance that pokes out can be cut off.

8 Fold the inside and outside of the bias tape to make a double layer. Place marks between the edge of the bias and the ⅝" (1.5cm) width of binding.

9 Align it with the edges of the quilt and keep it steady with marking pins. Sew it by backstitching through.

10 Sew until you're almost at the corner. Use a ruler to make a mark at the ⅝" (1.5cm) spot.

11 Sew until you reach your mark, then stop.

12 Fold the bias tape at a right angle, and align it with the next section. The corner will rise in a triangular shape, so also align the quilt's edges and the bias tape's pleat with it.

13 Insert the needle into the corner where you placed a mark; only pierce the bias tape, and make the needle exit again at its opposite side. Now continue sewing, backstitching the next section.

14 The end section of the bias tape must be placed so it overlaps ⅝" (1.5cm) over the starting section. If the bias is too long, make a diagonal cut of ⅝" (1.5cm), but not in its folded state. Make sure you first unfold it into one single piece before cutting.

15 Fold the bias tape back into the reverse of the fabric, wrap up the seam allowance, and keep it steady with marking pins to prevent the stitches from being visible. Blindstitch the folded section of bias.

16 Sew up to the edge of the quilt using a slip stitch. Tidy the corner by folding it at a 45-degree angle.

17 Once you've sewn up to the edge, return back through the inside of the fabric and make the needle exit again at the corner.

18 Wrap the seam allowance of the next section with bias tape and keep it still with marking pins. Fold the corner diagonally to align it.

19 Stitch the folded corner once and then pause.

20 Blindstitch the next section. Once you've blindstitched around the entire quilt, you're done.

How to do reverse appliqué

1 Prepare a base fabric (left) and a motif fabric (right). With reverse appliqué, the fabrics are placed in the reverse order to regular appliqué. This time, draw the sketch onto the base fabric.

2 Place the base fabric over the motif fabric and tack it. Appliqué as if you were hemming; tack by following the inside edges, following the sketch.

3 Cut out the sketch, always leaving a ⅛" (3mm) seam allowance. The motif fabric underneath will become visible now.

4 Blindstitch the motif fabric while inserting the seam allowances with marks. The appliqué technique used here is the same as "Doing appliqué: Basic slip stitch" on page 57.

How to make 3D flowers

I'll explain by using the three-dimensional lokelani flowers, as shown on page 34. You can also use these heart-shaped parts for the motifs on pages 50–53; however, some are different because of the spaces left open to turn right side out.

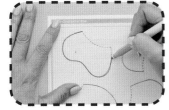

1 Create the parts for the flower petals. Turn that nonwoven fabric, the fusible web, so its sticky side is facing up and copy the sketch onto it. Once you've drawn all the flower petals, cut them by following the marks.

2 Stick the adhesive parts from step 1 onto the fabric you'll use for the flower petals. Fold the fabric inside out, and sew around the fusible web parts. The root of each petal will be where the open space will be left, so don't sew that part. Sew around the heart-shaped part of each petal without leaving any seam allowance. Don't sew the round circle.

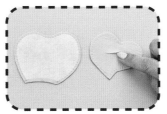

3 Add a ⅛" (3mm) seam allowance and cut out all the parts. Cut the round circle, which you didn't sew. Make a cut in the center of the nonstick part of the heart-shaped pieces' fusible web and leave an open space there.

4 Using the cut-open space, turn the heart-shaped pieces right side out. If you pull at the cloth with forceps, you can perfectly turn them inside out all way to the edges.

5 All the flower petal parts are done except for the round shape.

6 Now you'll make that central part. Prepare two square pieces with 2 ⅜" (6cm) sides and fold them both to create triangles. The long sides of each triangle will acquire bias, so straighten them with your fingers.

7 Place the triangles from step 6 onto the right side of the round shape—the side that doesn't have any fusible web on it. Place marking pins in such a way that the central section doesn't fully touch the round shape, so it's hovering above it.

8 Take the inside of the round shape, which does have fusible web on it, and place it on top.

9 Sew around the circumference of it. The excess seam allowance from the triangles can be cut.

10 Make a cut on the side of the round shape without fusible web. Turn right side out. The piled triangle parts will now float up slightly.

11 Insert some cotton for craft use into the cut to make it plump. Roughly stitch the cut back up to close it.

12 Place some tulle, or another transparent fabric, over the sketch. Join petals 1 to 5 (as marked on the pattern). Sew the base of each petal to the tulle to keep them attached.

13 Join petals 6 to 10 in that order. Sew them to keep them attached.

14 Place part 11, the round circle. Stitch it at two or three places from its wrong side, to prevent the seams on its front from being visible. Make sure it doesn't lose its sense of three-dimensionality in the process.

15 Cut the excess tulle to prevent it being visible from the front.

16 Your 3D flower is complete.

Fabric Shop

I will now introduce the fabrics I have been using in this book. For the hand-dyed fabric, it's perfectly okay if you buy plain fabrics (eighty square) from a craft store.

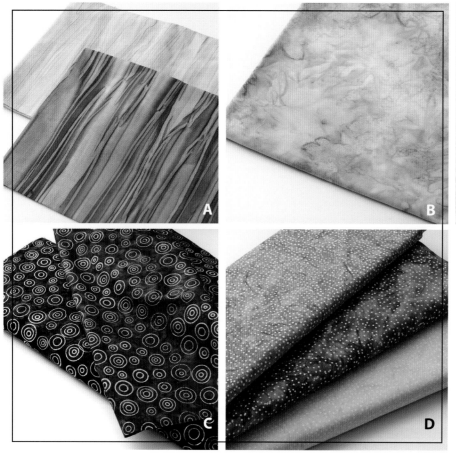

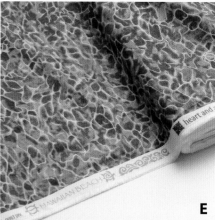

A–D Original batik: this is an easy-to-use material that can easily be given a multitude of uses, such as for base fabrics, motif fabrics, borders, or reverse materials. I manufactured these prints in joint production with the company Miu Mint Aloha.

E Original printed fabrics: they were created with Heart and Art specifically for ocean-themed quilts. Small green sea turtles swim over a pattern depicting the glittering surface of the water.

Tie-dye: Tie-dye fabrics are easy to use as a base material or as the motif cloth for a reverse appliqué. They're all dyed by hand by Shades Textiles.

Hand-dyed fabrics: This is the plain fabric I always use, specially ordered from the artist Chihiro Yagi. The benefits to custom-ordering fabric are that you choose the color, and they dye it for you. This material is very easy to sew.

How to Make the Projects

- In most cases, the appliqué fabric will be sewn onto the base fabric as an appliqué.
- I add about ⅛" (3mm) of seam allowance to the appliqué fabric. If not indicated, add between ¼" to ⅜" (7.1 to 10mm) of seam allowance.
- After quilting, it all shrinks slightly, so add a little extra seam allowance to the entire border. Once the quilting is done, cut it at the exact measurement. You can even quilt outside the limits of your border to account for possible shrinking.
- Make sure to refer to the quilting lessons that begin on page 56.
- When copying the sketch, if you're using a fabric with a pale color, it's okay to place the sketch underneath and trace it.
- When doing appliqué, don't cut it all at once. Attach the appliqué fabric to the base fabric with tacking first. Then start making cuts little by little, blindstitching them one after the other.
- The large patterns are found at the end; however, some small patterns are paired with the project. Before using the pattern paper, please follow the instructions, such as expanding the image at the specified percentage.
- I introduced specialty fabrics on page 62, but you can use whatever fabrics you like.
- For embroidery threads, I sew a double strand if I'm using a #25 thickness. Sometimes I also use a #12 thickness. Please use a thread thickness that you feel comfortable with.
- I use piping cord bought at a store, but it's okay to make your own, too. On each instruction page, remember to consult the materials list and the exact measurements.
- I've given slightly large sizes for every fabric on the materials lists. Especially for binding, this allows for the possibility of not sewing it super finely and it still turning out okay.
- Instructions for a half-backstitch: stitch in the same way as a typical backstitch, but after one stitch, go back only halfway through the stitch. Next, the needle is released twice as far ahead as the stitch, and the stitch is returned half again. Repeat the process.

Materials

Base fabric: 43¼" x 43¼" (110 x 110cm)
Appliqué fabric (navy blue): 43¼" x 43¼" (110 x 110cm)
Appliqué fabric (white): 23⅔" x 23⅔" (60 x 60cm)
Cotton batting: 43¼" x 43¼" (110 x 110cm)*
Backing fabric: 43¼" x 43¼" (110 x 110cm)*
Binding fabric: 39⅜" x 43¼" (100 x 110cm)

Instructions

1) Take care of the appliqué and complete the top section.
2) Sandwich the top over the cotton batting and the backing, tack them, and start quilting.
3) Keep the border contained with double binding.

* Note: To ensure your backing and batting remain large enough to accommodate the quilt front following the quilting process, you may prefer to cut 10" (25.4cm) both wider and longer than your finished project dimensions. Trim after quilting.

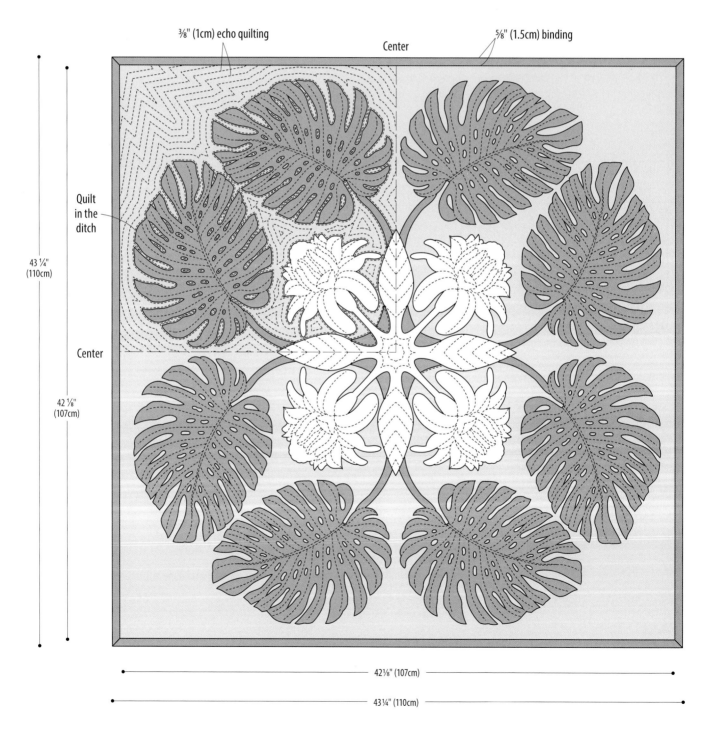

⅜" (1cm) echo quilting

⅝" (1.5cm) binding

Center

Quilt in the ditch

Center

43 ¼" (110cm)

42 ⅛" (107cm)

42⅛" (107cm)

43¼" (110cm)

Materials

Base fabric: 25⅝" x 15¾" (65 x 40cm)
Appliqué fabric: 25⅝" x 15¾" (65 x 40cm)
Cotton batting: 25⅝" x 15¾" (65 x 40cm)*
Backing fabric: 25⅝" x 15¾" (65 x 40cm)*
Frame (inner dimensions): 21" x 12½" (53.5 x 31.5cm)

Instructions

1) Take care of the appliqué and complete the top section.
2) Sandwich the top over the cotton batting and the backing, tack them, and start quilting.
3) Crop it to the final size.
4) Insert in the frame.

* **Note:** To ensure your backing and batting remain large enough to accommodate the quilt front following the quilting process, you may prefer to cut 6" (15.2cm) both wider and longer than your finished project dimensions. Trim after quilting.

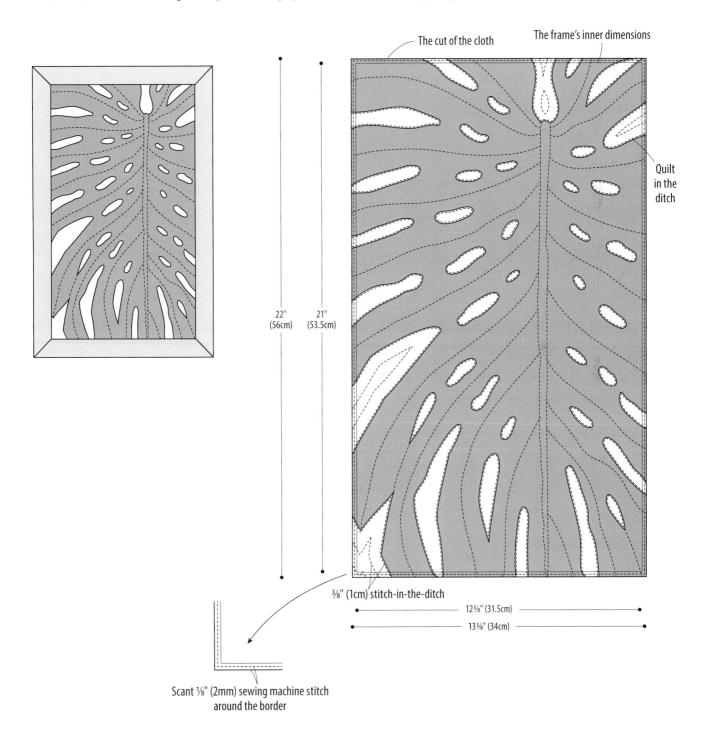

The cut of the cloth

The frame's inner dimensions

Quilt in the ditch

22" (56cm)

21" (53.5cm)

⅜" (1cm) stitch-in-the-ditch

12⅜" (31.5cm)

13⅜" (34cm)

Scant ⅛" (2mm) sewing machine stitch around the border

Materials

Base fabric: 19⅔" x 19⅔" (50 x 50cm)
Appliqué fabric: 19⅔" x 19⅔" (50 x 50cm)
Main body fabric (for back): 19⅔" x 27½" (50 x 70cm)
Cotton batting: 19⅔" x 19⅔" (50 x 50cm)*
Backing fabric: 19⅔" x 19⅔" (50 x 50cm)*
Cushion insert(s): 17¾" x 17¾" (45 x 45cm) each

Instructions

1) Take care of the appliqué and complete the top section.
2) Sandwich the top over the cotton batting and the backing, tack them, and start quilting.
3) Create the back of the main body.
4) Join the front and back of the main body. Sew them.
5) Finish the seam allowance, turn right side out, and insert the cushion.

* Note: To ensure your backing and batting remain large enough to accommodate the quilt front following the quilting process, you may prefer to cut 6" (15.2cm) both wider and longer than your finished project dimensions. Trim after quilting.

A. Front (one piece)

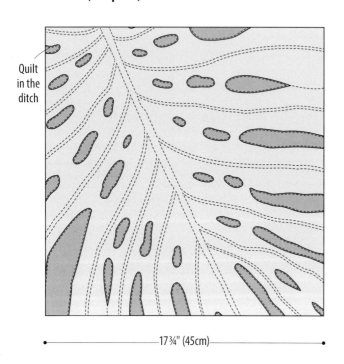

Quilt in the ditch

17¾" (45cm)

B. Front (one piece)

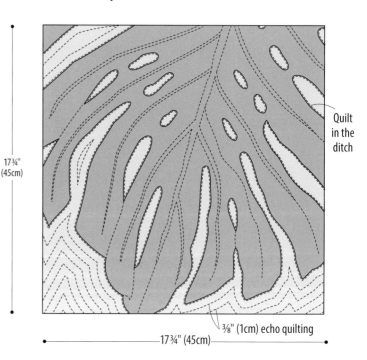

17¾" (45cm)

Quilt in the ditch

⅜" (1cm) echo quilting

17¾" (45cm)

Back (two pieces)

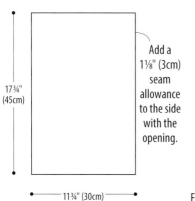

17¾" (45cm)

Add a 1⅛" (3cm) seam allowance to the side with the opening.

11¾" (30cm)

How to Make the Back

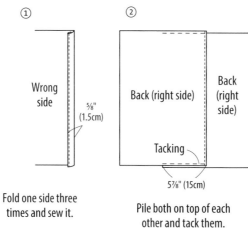

① Wrong side

⅝" (1.5cm)

Fold one side three times and sew it.

② Back (right side)   Back (right side)

Tacking

5⅞" (15cm)

Pile both on top of each other and tack them.

How to Sew

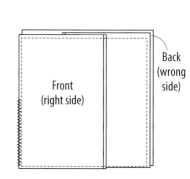

Front (right side)

Back (wrong side)

Join the front and back and sew the edges together. Turn right side out, and finish the seam allowance with a zigzag stitch or with bias tape.

Materials

Base fabric: 67" x 43¼" (170 x 110cm)

Appliqué fabric (includes binding): 106⅓" x 43¼" (270 x 110cm)

Cotton batting: 67" x 43¼" (170 x 110cm)*

Backing fabric: 67" x 43¼" (170 x 110cm)*

Thick embroidery thread: as needed

Instructions

1) Take care of the appliqué and complete the top section.
2) Sandwich the top over the cotton batting and the backing, tack them, and start quilting as well as embroidering.
3) Seal around the edges with double binding.

* **Note:** To ensure your backing and batting remain large enough to accommodate the quilt front following the quilting process, you may prefer to cut 10" (25.4cm) both wider and longer than your finished project dimensions. Trim after quilting.

How to Sew a Backstitch

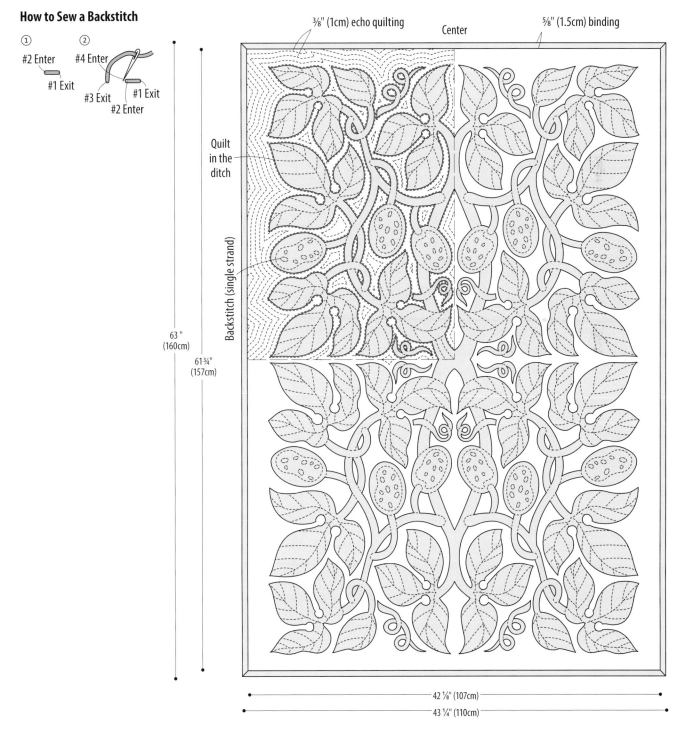

① #2 Enter #1 Exit

② #4 Enter #3 Exit #2 Enter #1 Exit

⅜" (1cm) echo quilting   Center   ⅝" (1.5cm) binding

Quilt in the ditch

Backstitch (single strand)

63" (160cm)

61¾" (157cm)

42⅛" (107cm)

43¼" (110cm)

Materials

Bottom fabric: 15¾" x 35⅜" (40 x 90cm)
Appliqué fabric: 11¾" x 35⅜" (30 x 90cm)
Cotton batting: 15¾" x 35⅜" (40 x 90cm)
Backing fabric: 15¾" x 35⅜" (40 x 90cm)
Lining fabric: 15¾" x 29½" (40 x 75cm)
Store-bought handle: 25⅝" x 1½" (65 x 4cm)

Bottom (one piece)

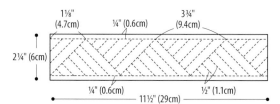

1⅛" (4.7cm)   ¼" (0.6cm)   3¾" (9.4cm)
2¼" (6cm)
¼" (0.6cm)   ½" (1.1cm)
11½" (29cm)

Main Body (one piece each)   **Note:** Left and right are inverted.

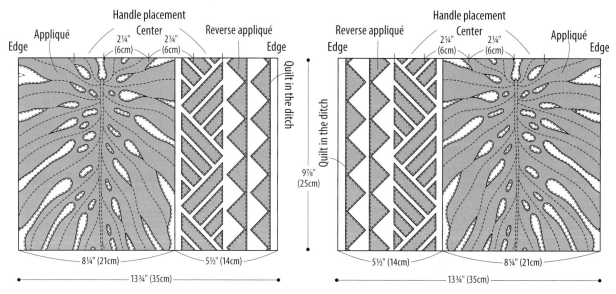

Edge   Appliqué   Handle placement   Center   2¼" (6cm)   2¼" (6cm)   Reverse appliqué   Edge
Quilt in the ditch
Quilt in the ditch
9⅞" (25cm)
8¼" (21cm)   5½" (14cm)
13¾" (35cm)

Reverse appliqué   Edge   Handle placement   Center   2¼" (6cm)   2¼" (6cm)   Appliqué   Edge
5½" (14cm)   8¼" (21cm)
13¾" (35cm)

Lining (one piece)

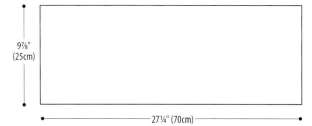

9⅞" (25cm)
27¼" (70cm)

Bottom of Lining (one piece)

2¼" (6cm)
11½" (29cm)

How to Make the Main Body

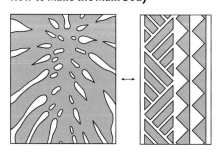

Create each pattern separately
and then unite them.

Instructions

1) Take care of the appliqué and complete the top section for the main body. The bottom's top section will be one piece of fabric.
2) Sandwich the top over the cotton batting and the backing, tack them, and start quilting as well as embroidering.
3) Fold the main body at the middle. Unite the edges and sew them.
4) Join the bottom with the main body and sew them together.
5) Sew the lining in the same way as the bag.
6) Temporarily attach the handle to the main body. Fit the lining into the bag. Sew the opening.
7) Turn right side out and close the space left open. Fit the lining into place with a cover stitch.

How to Make the Lining

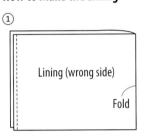

① Bring together the two pieces of lining. Sew to create a loop.

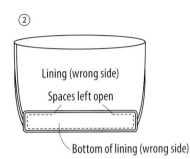

② Unite the lining and the bottom lining, then sew them together.

How to Attach the Handle

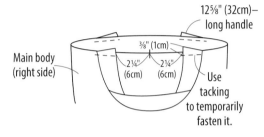

Attach it diagonally to the opening on the main body. To make your own handle, see page 99.

How to Sew the Bag

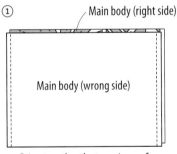

① Bring together the two pieces of the main body. Sew both edges.

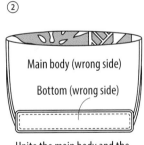

② Unite the main body and bottom, then sew them together.

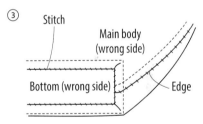

③ Fold the seam allowance's edge to its side and fold the bottom to the bottom's side. Stitch them.

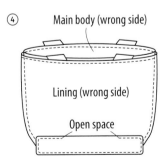

④ Temporarily fasten the handle to the main body. Unite the lining with the main body and sew.

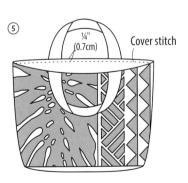

⑤ Turn the bag right side out. Close the open space with a whipstitch, and seal the lining with a cover stitch.

Materials

Base fabric: 11¾" x 43¼" (30 x 110cm)
Appliqué fabric: 11¾" x 43¼" (30 x 110cm)
Cotton batting: 11¾" x 43¼" (30 x 110cm)
Backing fabric: 11¾" x 43¼" (30 x 110cm)
Lining fabric (includes pockets): 19⅔" x 43¼" (50 x 110cm)

Piping cord fabric: 15¾" x 19⅔" (40 x 50cm)
Store-bought flat tape (for handles): 41⅓" x 1⅛" (105 x 3cm)
Thick embroidery thread: as needed
Piping cord: as needed

Main Body (two pieces)

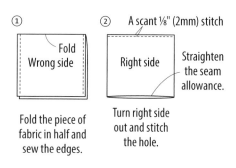

Location for the handle
Center
Edge   3" (7.5cm)   3" (7.5cm)   Edge
⅜" (1cm) echo quilting
9⅞" (25cm)
Quilt in the ditch
Backstitch (single strand)
19⅔" (50cm)

How to Make the Piping Cord

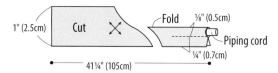

1" (2.5cm)   Cut   ⅛" (0.5cm)   Fold
Piping cord
¼" (0.7cm)
41¼" (105cm)

Note: You can also buy ready-made piping from a store.

Lining (two pieces)

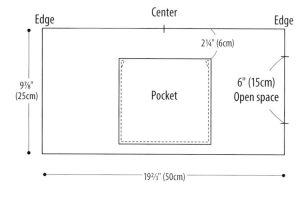

Edge   Center   Edge
2¼" (6cm)
9⅞" (25cm)   Pocket   6" (15cm) Open space
19⅔" (50cm)

Pocket (one piece)

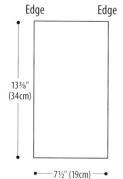

Edge   Edge
13⅜" (34cm)
7½" (19cm)

How to Make the Pocket

① Fold   Wrong side
Fold the piece of fabric in half and sew the edges.

② A scant ⅛" (2mm) stitch
Right side
Straighten the seam allowance.
Turn right side out and stitch the hole.

How to Attach the Handle

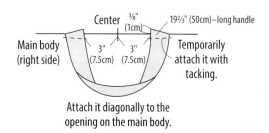

Center   ⅜" (1cm)   19⅔" (50cm)–long handle
Main body (right side)   3" (7.5cm)   3" (7.5cm)   Temporarily attach it with tacking.
Attach it diagonally to the opening on the main body.

Instructions

1) Take care of the appliqué and complete the top section of the main body.
2) Sandwich the top over the cotton batting and the backing, tack them, and start quilting as well as embroidering.
3) Create some piping cord and use a sewing machine to attach it to the edges of the main body.
4) Fold the main body in two and sew the joined edges.
5) Create the pocket and attach it to the lining. Then sew the lining.
6) Temporarily attach the handle to the main body. Join the lining to the main body and sew the opening.
7) Turn right side out, close the open space, and seal it with a cover stitch. You can add a magnet button if you wish, too.

Instructions

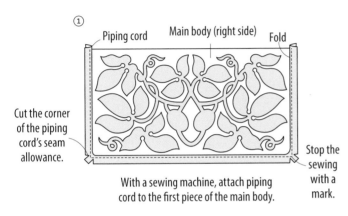

① Piping cord — Main body (right side) — Fold

Cut the corner of the piping cord's seam allowance.

Stop the sewing with a mark.

With a sewing machine, attach piping cord to the first piece of the main body.

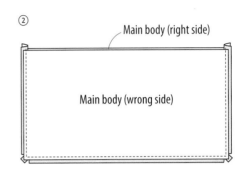

② Main body (right side)

Main body (wrong side)

Join both pieces of the main body and sew them at the edges. Leave an open space in the edges of the lining and sew it in the same way as the main body, without interfering with the piping cord

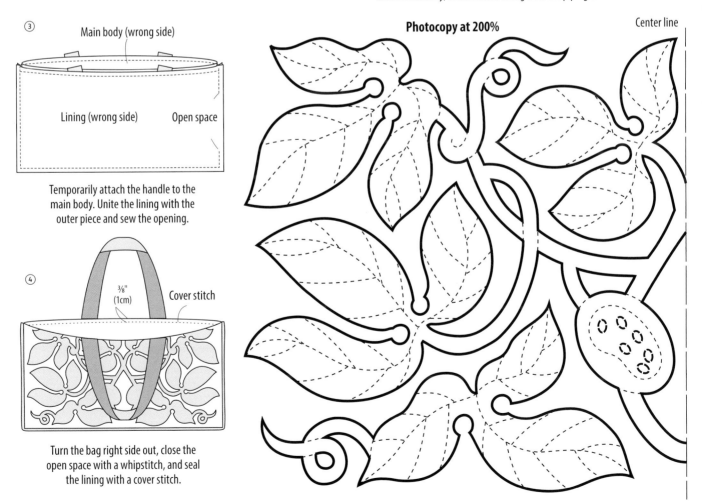

③ Main body (wrong side)

Lining (wrong side)   Open space

Temporarily attach the handle to the main body. Unite the lining with the outer piece and sew the opening.

④ ³⁄₈" (1cm) Cover stitch

Turn the bag right side out, close the open space with a whipstitch, and seal the lining with a cover stitch.

Photocopy at 200%   Center line

See pattern on page 115

Materials

Base fabric: 31½" x 19⅔" (80 x 50cm)
Appliqué fabric: 25⅝" x 15¾" (65 x 40cm)
Cotton batting: 31½" x 19⅔" (80 x 50cm)*
Backing fabric: 31½" x 19⅔" (80 x 50cm)*
Frame (inner dimensions): 16⅔" x 27¼" (42.3 x 69.3cm)
Canvas (inner dimensions): 13" x 23⅔" (33 x 60cm)
Thick embroidery thread: as needed

Instructions

1) Take care of the appliqué and complete the top section.
2) Sandwich the top over the cotton batting and the backing, tack them, and start quilting as well as embroidering.
3) Crop it to fit the final size.
4) Insert the quilt into the frame.

* **Note:** To ensure your backing and batting remain large enough to accommodate the quilt front following the quilting process, you may prefer to cut 6" (15.2cm) both wider and longer than your finished project dimensions. Trim after quilting.

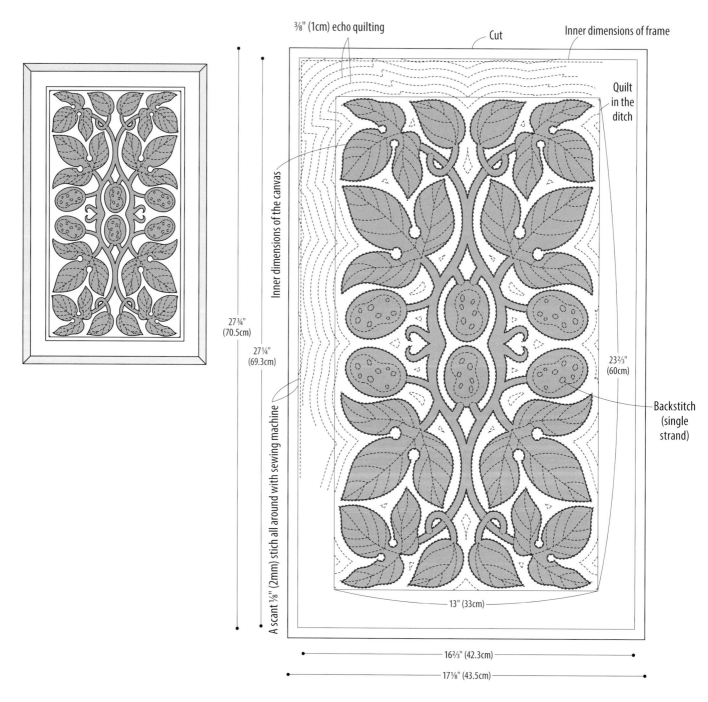

⅜" (1cm) echo quilting

Cut

Inner dimensions of frame

Quilt in the ditch

Inner dimensions of the canvas

27¾" (70.5cm)

27¼" (69.3cm)

A scant ⅛" (2mm) stitch all around with sewing machine

23⅔" (60cm)

Backstitch (single strand)

13" (33cm)

16⅔" (42.3cm)

17⅛" (43.5cm)

08 Threefold Lilikoi Case

See pattern on page 115

Materials

Base fabric: 9⅞" x 15¾"
(25 x 40cm)

Appliqué fabric: 9⅞" x 15¾"
(25 x 40cm)

Cotton batting: 9⅞" x 15¾"
(25 x 40cm)

Backing fabric: 9⅞" x 15¾"
(25 x 40cm)

Lining fabric: 9⅞" x 15¾"
(25 x 40cm)

Button: 1 1/16" (2.7cm) diameter

Support button:
⅜" (1cm) diameter

Leather cord: 1/32" (1mm)
diameter x 43¼" (110cm) long

Thick embroidery thread:
as needed

Instructions

1) Take care of the appliqué and complete the top section of the main body.
2) Sandwich the top over the cotton batting and the backing, tack them, and start quilting as well as embroidering.
3) Fold the main body and the lining by the middle, leave an open space, and sew them. Turn the case right side out and close it.
4) Fold the bottom at its center and close both sides with a whipstitch.
5) Attach the buttons and the leather cord.

Main Body (one piece)

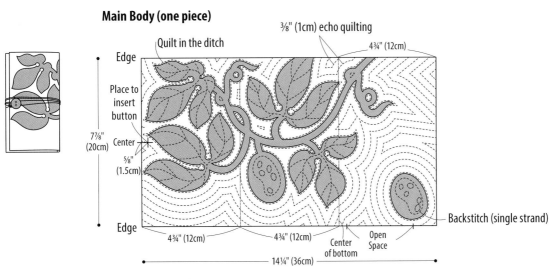

Lining (one piece)

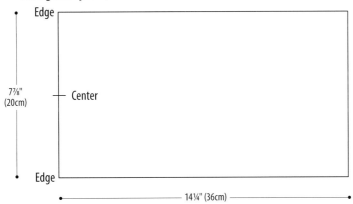

Instructions

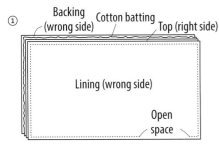

Join the main body and the lining by the middle. Sew all around them but leave an open space.

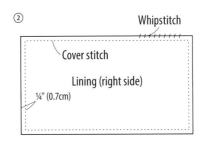

Turn right side out and secure the open space by closing it with a whipstitch. Sew a cover stitch to prevent it from affecting the rest of the quilt.

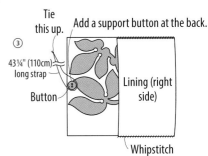

Fold the fabric at the center of the bottom. Pierce the main body and secure it with a whipstitch. Attach the button and the strap.

Materials

Base fabric: 27½" x 59" (70 x 150cm)
Appliqué fabric (blue): 27½" x 59" (70 x 150cm)
Appliqué fabric (pea green): 19⅔" x 8" (50 x 20cm)
Cotton batting: 27½" x 59" (70 x 150cm)*
Backing fabric: 27½" x 59" (70 x 150cm)*
3 stretched canvases: 21¼" x 15" (54 x 38cm)

Instructions

1) Take care of the appliqué and complete the top section.
2) Sandwich the top over the cotton batting and the backing, tack them, and start quilting.
3) Add the stretched canvas on top and wrap around them, then stick them on with tape.

* **Note:** To ensure your backing and batting remain large enough to accommodate the quilt front following the quilting process, you may prefer to cut 6" (15.2cm) both wider and longer than your finished project dimensions. Trim after quilting.

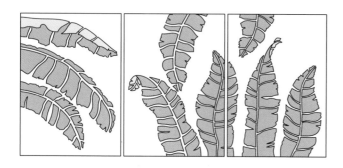

Instructions

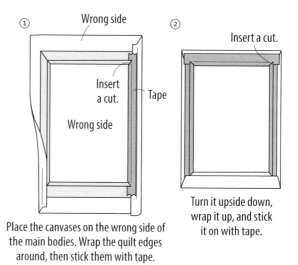

① Place the canvases on the wrong side of the main bodies. Wrap the quilt edges around, then stick them with tape.

② Turn it upside down, wrap it up, and stick it on with tape.

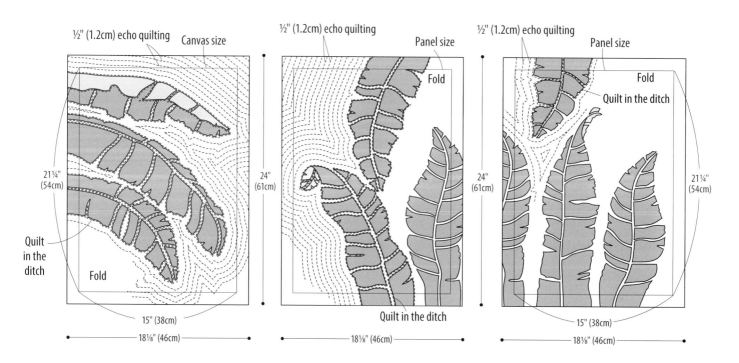

Stitched Banana Leaf Tote Bag   See pattern on page 117

Materials

Main body fabric (includes facing): 43¼" x 17¾" (110 x 45cm)

Lining fabric (includes pocket): 43¼" x 17¾" (110 x 45cm)

Fusible web: 43¼" x 17¾" (110 x 45cm)

Leather strap (for handle): 27½" x 1½" (70cm x 4cm)

Plastic insert (for bottom of bag): 7⅞" x 9⅞" (20 x 25cm)

Thick embroidery thread: as needed

Instructions

1) Embroider the main body and stick fusible web to the wrong side.

2) Fold the main body in two and sew the edges and gussets together.

3) Create the pocket and then attach it to the lining. Then sew lining.

4) Temporarily attach the handle onto the main body, fold the lining, and sew the opening.

5) Turn the bag right side out, insert the bottom plate, close the open space, and stitch the bag opening to keep it in place.

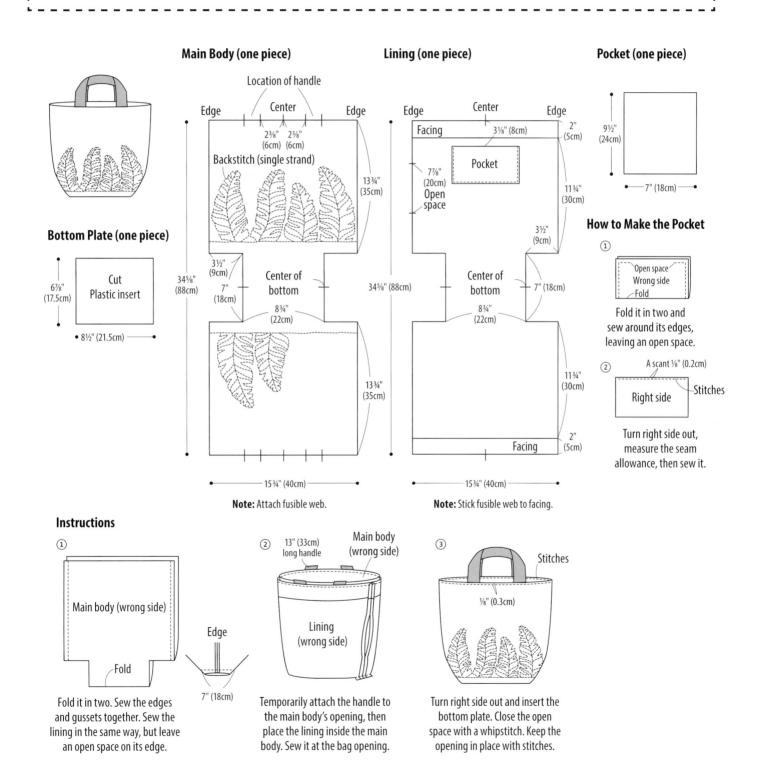

Main Body (one piece)

Location of handle — Center
Edge / Edge
2⅜" (6cm) / 2⅜" (6cm)
Backstitch (single strand)
13¾" (35cm)
34⅝" (88cm)
3½" (9cm)
7" (18cm)
Center of bottom
8¾" (22cm)
13¾" (35cm)
15¾" (40cm)
Note: Attach fusible web.

Lining (one piece)

Edge — Center — Edge
Facing
3⅛" (8cm) / 2" (5cm)
7⅞" (20cm) Open space
Pocket
11¾" (30cm)
3½" (9cm)
7" (18cm)
34⅝" (88cm)
Center of bottom
8¾" (22cm)
11¾" (30cm)
2" (5cm)
Facing
15¾" (40cm)
Note: Stick fusible web to facing.

Pocket (one piece)

9½" (24cm)
7" (18cm)

How to Make the Pocket

① Open space / Wrong side / Fold

Fold it in two and sew around its edges, leaving an open space.

② A scant ⅛" (0.2cm)
Right side — Stitches

Turn right side out, measure the seam allowance, then sew it.

Bottom Plate (one piece)

6⅞" (17.5cm)
Cut Plastic insert
8½" (21.5cm)

Instructions

① Main body (wrong side)
Fold
Edge
7" (18cm)

Fold it in two. Sew the edges and gussets together. Sew the lining in the same way, but leave an open space on its edge.

② 13" (33cm) long handle
Main body (wrong side)
Lining (wrong side)

Temporarily attach the handle to the main body's opening, then place the lining inside the main body. Sew it at the bag opening.

③ Stitches
⅛" (0.3cm)

Turn right side out and insert the bottom plate. Close the open space with a whipstitch. Keep the opening in place with stitches.

Materials

Main body fabric: 11¾" x 9⅞" (30 x 25cm)
Lining fabric: 11¾" x 9⅞" (30 x 25cm)
Fusible web: 11¾" x 9⅞" (30 x 25cm)
Zipper: 7⅞" (20cm)
Thick embroidery thread: as needed

Instructions

1) Embroider the main body and stick fusible web to the wrong side.
2) Unite the main body and the lining by the middle, sandwiching the zipper. Sew the bag opening.
3) Fold the main body with itself and the lining with itself. Sew the edges together, leaving an open space in the lining.
4) Turn right side out and seal the open space.

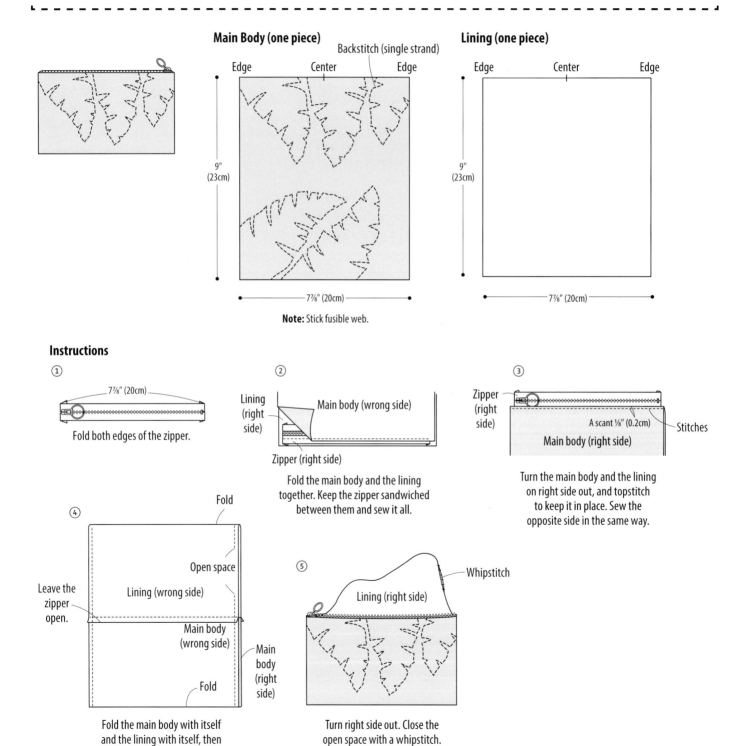

Main Body (one piece)

Backstitch (single strand)

Edge   Center   Edge

9" (23cm)

7⅞" (20cm)

Note: Stick fusible web.

Lining (one piece)

Edge   Center   Edge

9" (23cm)

7⅞" (20cm)

Instructions

① 7⅞" (20cm)
Fold both edges of the zipper.

② Lining (right side) Main body (wrong side)
Zipper (right side)
Fold the main body and the lining together. Keep the zipper sandwiched between them and sew it all.

③ Zipper (right side)
A scant ⅛" (0.2cm)   Stitches
Main body (right side)
Turn the main body and the lining on right side out, and topstitch to keep it in place. Sew the opposite side in the same way.

④ Fold
Open space
Lining (wrong side)
Leave the zipper open.
Main body (wrong side)
Main body (right side)
Fold
Fold the main body with itself and the lining with itself, then sew the edges together, leaving an open space in the lining.

⑤ Whipstitch
Lining (right side)
Turn right side out. Close the open space with a whipstitch.

Materials

Base fabric: 67" x 43¼" (170 x 110cm)
Appliqué fabric (includes binding): 106⅓" x 43¼" (270 x 110cm)
Cotton batting: 67" x 43¼" (170 x 110cm)*
Backing fabric: 67" x 43¼" (170 x 110cm)*

Instructions

1) Take care of the appliqué and complete the top section.
2) Sandwich the top over the cotton batting and the backing, tack them, and start quilting.
3) Keep the border contained with double binding.

* **Note:** To ensure your backing and batting remain large enough to accommodate the quilt front following the quilting process, you may prefer to cut 10" (25.4cm) both wider and longer than your finished project dimensions. Trim after quilting.

⅝" (1.5cm) binding

Center

⅜" (1cm) echo quilting

Quilt in the ditch

61¾" (157cm)

63" (160cm)

Center

42 ⅛" (107cm)

43 ¼" (110cm)

Materials

Base fabric: 23⅔" x 23⅔" (60 x 60cm)
Appliqué fabric: 23⅔" x 23⅔" (60 x 60cm)
Cotton batting: 23⅔" x 23⅔" (60 x 60cm)*
Backing fabric: 23⅔" x 23⅔" (60 x 60cm)*
Binding fabric: 21⅔" x 39⅜" (55 x 100cm)

Instructions

1) Take care of the appliqué and complete the top section.
2) Sandwich the top over the cotton batting and the backing, tack them, and start quilting.
3) Keep the border contained with double binding.

Note: For more detailed instructions, see page 56

* **Note:** To ensure your backing and batting remain large enough to accommodate the quilt front following the quilting process, you may prefer to cut 6" (15.2cm) both wider and longer than your finished project dimensions. Trim after quilting.

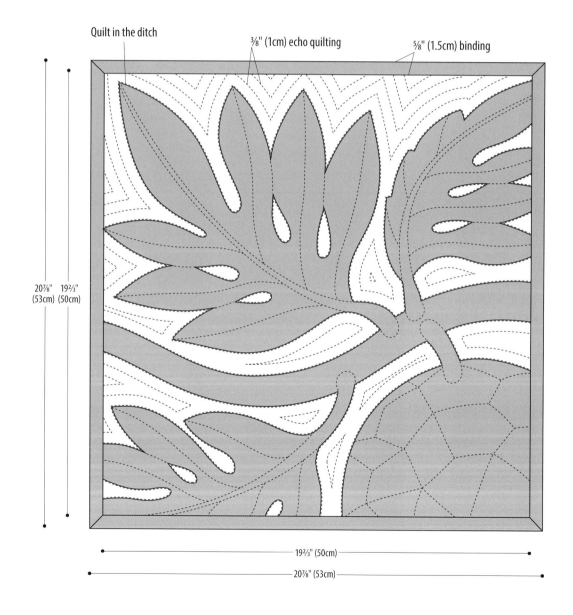

Quilt in the ditch

⅜" (1cm) echo quilting

⅝" (1.5cm) binding

20⅞" (53cm)   19⅔" (50cm)

19⅔" (50cm)

20⅞" (53cm)

Materials

Base fabric: 19⅔" x 19⅔" (50 x 50cm)

Appliqué fabric: 19⅔" x 19⅔" (50 x 50cm)

Main body fabric (for back): 19⅔" x 27½" (50 x 70cm)

Cotton batting: 19⅔" x 19⅔" (50 x 50cm)*

Backing fabric: 19⅔" x 19⅔" (50 x 50cm)*

Cushion insert: 17¾" x 17¾" (45 x 45cm)

Instructions

1) Take care of the appliqué and complete the top section.
2) Sandwich the top over the cotton batting and the backing, tack them, and start quilting.
3) Create the back of the main body.
4) Join the back and front of the main body and sew them.
5) Finish the seam allowance, turn right side out, and insert the cushion.

* Note: To ensure your backing and batting remain large enough to accommodate the quilt front following the quilting process, you may prefer to cut 6" (15.2cm) both wider and longer than your finished project dimensions. Trim after quilting.

A. Front of Main Body (one piece)

⅜" (1cm) echo quilting

Quilt in the ditch

17¾" (45cm)

B. Front of Main Body (one piece)

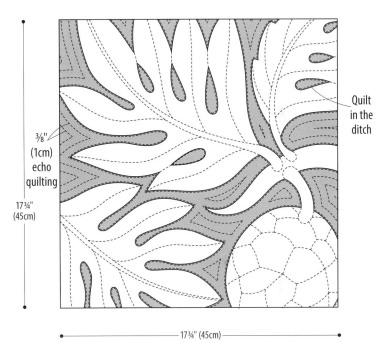

⅜" (1cm) echo quilting

Quilt in the ditch

17¾" (45cm)

17¾" (45cm)

Back of Main Body (two pieces)

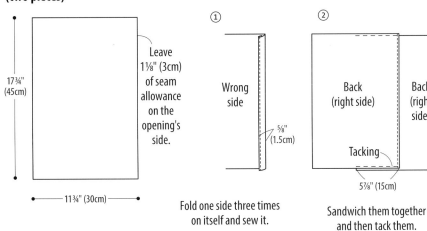

17¾" (45cm)

Leave 1⅛" (3cm) of seam allowance on the opening's side.

11¾" (30cm)

How to Make the Back of the Main Body

① Wrong side

⅝" (1.5cm)

Fold one side three times on itself and sew it.

② Back (right side)   Back (right side)

Tacking

5⅞" (15cm)

Sandwich them together and then tack them.

Instructions

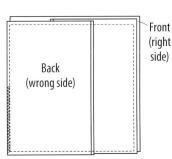

Back (wrong side)

Front (right side)

Join the main body's front and back together and sew them. Sew around the border and turn right side out. Finish the seam allowance by adding a zigzag stitch or wrapping around it with bias tape.

Materials

Base fabric: 90½" x 90½" (230 x 230cm)

Appliqué fabric: 82⅔" x 82⅔" (210 x 210cm)

Cotton batting: 90½" x 90½" (230 x 230cm)*

Backing fabric: 90½" x 90½" (230 x 230cm)*

Binding fabric: 70⅞" x 43¼" (180 x 110cm)

Instructions

1) Take care of the appliqué and complete the top section.

2) Sandwich the top over the cotton batting and the backing, tack them, and start quilting.

3) Keep the border contained with double binding.

* Note: To ensure your backing and batting remain large enough to accommodate the quilt front following the quilting process, you may prefer to cut 10" (25.4cm) both wider and longer than your finished project dimensions. Trim after quilting.

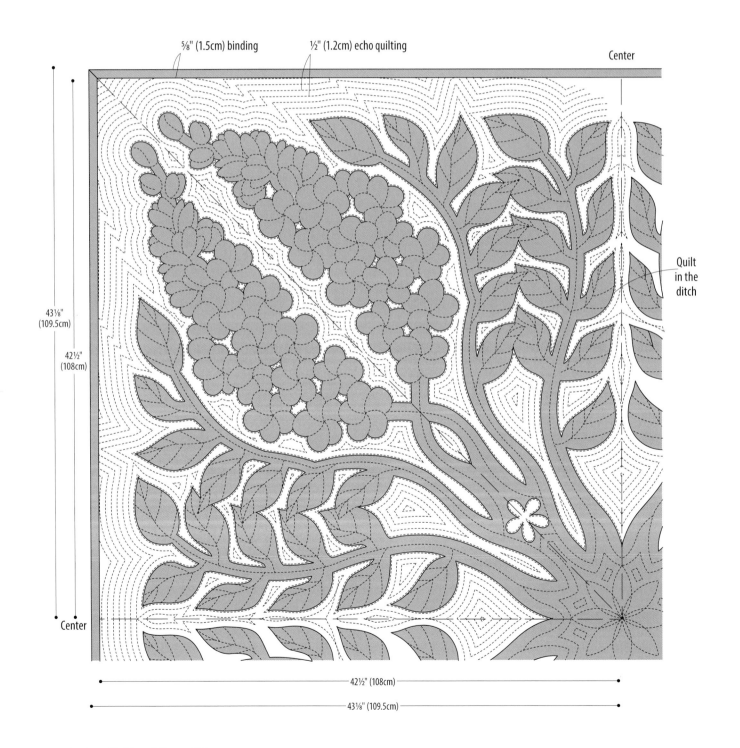

⅝" (1.5cm) binding   ½" (1.2cm) echo quilting   Center

Quilt in the ditch

43⅛" (109.5cm)

42½" (108cm)

Center

42½" (108cm)

43⅛" (109.5cm)

Materials

Base fabric (includes binding): 70⅞" x 43¼" (180 x 110cm)
Appliqué fabric: 43¼" x 43¼" (110 x 110cm)
Cotton batting: 43¼" x 43¼" (110 x 110cm)*
Backing fabric: 43¼" x 43¼" (110 x 110cm)*

Instructions

1) Take care of the appliqué and complete the top section.
2) Sandwich the top over the cotton batting and the backing, tack them, and start quilting.
3) Keep the border contained with double binding.

* **Note:** To ensure your backing and batting remain large enough to accommodate the quilt front following the quilting process, you may prefer to cut 10" (25.4cm) both wider and longer than your finished project dimensions. Trim after quilting.

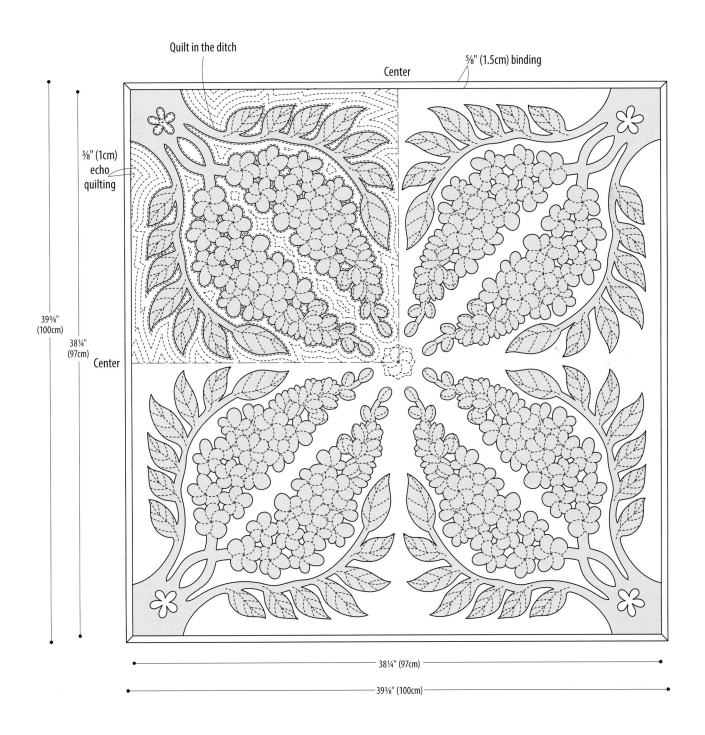

Materials

Base fabric (includes gusset): 21⅔" x 43¼" (55 x 110cm)
Appliqué fabric: 15¾" x 31½" (40 x 80cm)
Cotton batting: 21⅔" x 43¼" (55 x 110cm)
Backing fabric: 21⅔" x 43¼" (55 x 110cm)
Lining fabric (includes pocket): 21⅔" x 43¼" (55 x 110cm)

Piping cord fabric: 15¾" x 19⅔" (40 x 50cm)
Store-bought handle: 37⅜" x 1½" (95 x 4cm)
Plastic insert: 13¾" x 4" (35 x 10cm)
Thick embroidery thread: as needed
Piping cord: as needed

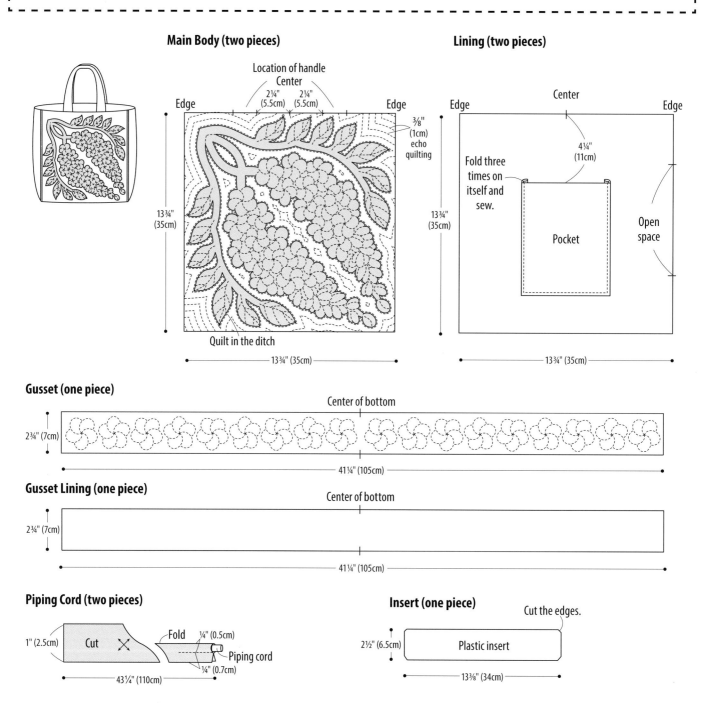

Main Body (two pieces)

Location of handle
Center
2¼" (5.5cm) 2¼" (5.5cm)

Edge   Edge

⅜" (1cm) echo quilting

13¾" (35cm)

Quilt in the ditch

13¾" (35cm)

Lining (two pieces)

Center

Edge   Edge

4¼" (11cm)

Fold three times on itself and sew.

Pocket

Open space

13¾" (35cm)

13¾" (35cm)

Gusset (one piece)

2¾" (7cm)

Center of bottom

41¼" (105cm)

Gusset Lining (one piece)

2¾" (7cm)

Center of bottom

41¼" (105cm)

Piping Cord (two pieces)

1" (2.5cm)

Cut

Fold

¼" (0.5cm)
Piping cord
¼" (0.7cm)

43¼" (110cm)

Insert (one piece)

Cut the edges.

2½" (6.5cm)

Plastic insert

13⅜" (34cm)

Note: You can also buy ready-made piping from a store.

Instructions

1) Take care of the appliqué and complete the top section of the main body. The gusset's top should be a single piece.
2) Sandwich the top over the cotton batting and the backing, tack them, and start quilting.
3) Create your piping cord. Sew it onto both edges of the gusset with a sewing machine.
4) Join the main body and the gusset together and sew them.
5) Create the pocket and attach it to the lining. Sew the lining.
6) Temporarily attach the handle to the main body, fold the lining together, and sew it.
7) Turn right side out, close the opening, and keep the lining in place with a cover stitch.

Pocket (one piece)

7" (18cm)

5⅞" (15cm)

How to Make the Pocket

¼" (2cm)

Wrong side

Fold the pocket top over three times and sew it.

How to Attach the Handle

Center
⅜" (1cm)
18½" (47cm) long handle

Main body (right side)

2¼" (5.5cm)   2¼" (5.5cm)

Temporarily attach with tacking.

Join it diagonally against the main body and sew it. To make your own handle, see page 99.

How to Integrate the Gusset

Piping cord

Fold

Fold

Gusset (right side)

Sew piping cord onto both sides of the gusset with a sewing machine.

Instructions

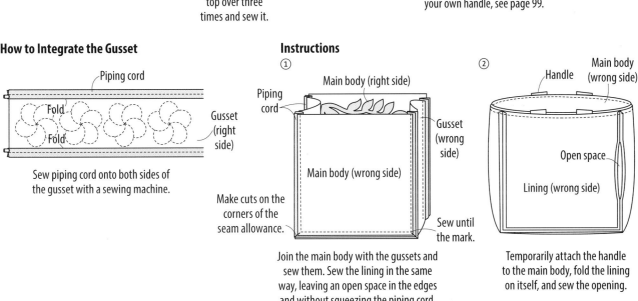

①
Piping cord

Main body (right side)

Gusset (wrong side)

Main body (wrong side)

Make cuts on the corners of the seam allowance.

Sew until the mark.

Join the main body with the gussets and sew them. Sew the lining in the same way, leaving an open space in the edges and without squeezing the piping cord.

②
Handle

Main body (wrong side)

Open space

Lining (wrong side)

Temporarily attach the handle to the main body, fold the lining on itself, and sew the opening.

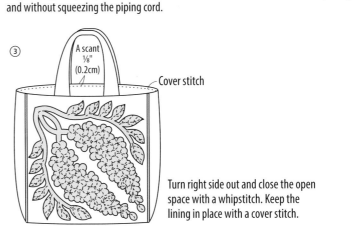

③
A scant ⅛" (0.2cm)

Cover stitch

Turn right side out and close the open space with a whipstitch. Keep the lining in place with a cover stitch.

Materials

Base fabric: 9⅞" x 27½"
(25 x 70cm)

Appliqué fabric: 7⅞" x 25⅝"
(20 x 65cm)

Cotton batting: 9⅞" x 27½"
(25 x 70cm)

Backing fabric: 9⅞" x 27½"
(25 x 70cm)

Lining fabric (includes pocket):
9⅞" x 29½" (25 x 75cm)

Piping cord fabric: 15¾" x 15¾"
(40 x 40cm)

Zipper: 11¾" (30cm)

Thick embroidery thread:
as needed

Piping cord: as needed

Instructions

1) Take care of the appliqué and complete the top section of the main body.
2) Sandwich the top over the cotton batting and the backing, tack them, and start quilting.
3) Create your piping cord and sew it onto the edges of the main body with a sewing machine.
4) Fold the main body together and sew it.
5) Create the pocket and attach it to the lining, then sew the lining.
6) Fold the opening and sew the zipper on.
7) Insert the lining into the main body and then blindstitch it to the zipper.

Main Body (two pieces)

Note: Mirror them left and right.

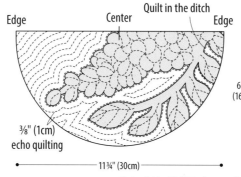
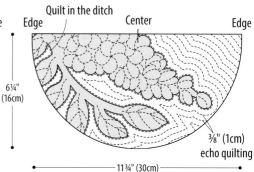

Edge   Center   Quilt in the ditch   Edge

⅜" (1cm) echo quilting

6¼" (16cm)

11¾" (30cm)

Note: Add a ⅝" (1.5cm) seam allowance on the opening.

Pocket (one piece)

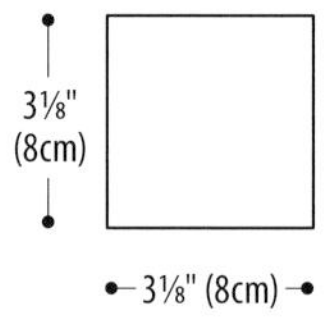

3⅛" (8cm)

3⅛" (8cm)

How to Make the Pocket

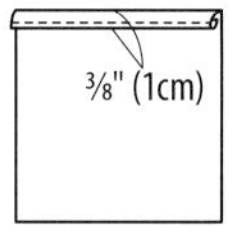

⅜" (1cm)

Fold the pocket top over three times and sew it.

Lining (two pieces)

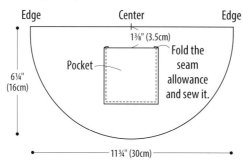

Edge   Center   Edge

1⅜" (3.5cm)

Pocket

Fold the seam allowance and sew it.

6¼" (16cm)

11¾" (30cm)

Piping Cord (one piece)

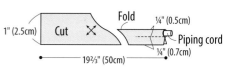

1" (2.5cm)   Cut   Fold

¼" (0.5cm)

Piping cord

¼" (0.7cm)

19⅔" (50cm)

Note: You can also buy ready-made piping from a store.

How to Sew a Half-Backstitch

Note: See page 63 for full instructions.

Instructions

①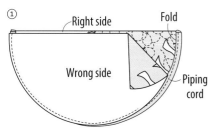

Right side   Fold

Wrong side

Piping cord

Use a sewing machine to sew the piping cord onto one piece of the main body. Join the other piece of the main body onto the first one and sew them. Sew the lining in the same way but being careful not to squash the piping cord.

②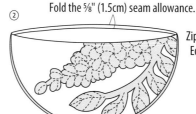

Fold the ⅝" (1.5cm) seam allowance.

Turn right side out and fold the opening's seam allowance.

③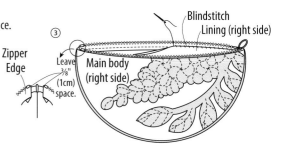

Blindstitch

Lining (right side)

Zipper Edge

Leave ⅜" (1cm) space.

Main body (right side)

Use a half-backstitch to sew the zipper onto the main body's opening. Insert the lining and blindstitch it on.

Materials

Base fabric: 67" x 43¼" (170 x 110cm)
Appliqué cloth (includes binding): 106⅓" x 43¼" (270 x 110cm)
Cotton batting: 67" x 43¼" (170 x 110cm)*
Backing fabric: 67" x 43¼" (170 x 110cm)*

Instructions

1) Take care of the appliqué and complete the top section.
2) Sandwich the top over the cotton batting and the backing, tack them, and start quilting.
3) Keep the border contained with double binding.

* **Note:** To ensure your backing and batting remain large enough to accommodate the quilt front following the quilting process, you may prefer to cut 10" (25.4cm) both wider and longer than your finished project dimensions. Trim after quilting.

½" (1.2cm) echo quilting   Center   ⅝" (1.5cm) binding

Quilt in the ditch

63" (160cm)

61¾" (157cm)

Center

42 ⅛" (107cm)

43 ¼" (110cm)

Materials

Base fabric: 17¾" x 9⅞" (45 x 25cm)

Appliqué fabric (for flower): 11¾" x 7⅞" (30 x 20cm)

Appliqué fabric (for stem): 15¾" x 9⅞" (40 x 25cm)

Border fabric: 17¾" x 13¾" (45 x 35cm)

Cotton batting: 23⅔" x 15¾" (60 x 40cm)*

Backing fabric: 23⅔" x 15¾" (60 x 40cm)*

3D flower fabric: 23⅔" x 11¾" (60 x 30cm)

Fusible web: 11¾" x 11¾" (30 x 30cm)

Tulle: 4" x 4" (10 x 10cm)

Craft cotton: as needed

Thick embroidery thread: as needed

* **Note:** To ensure your backing and batting remain large enough to accommodate the quilt front following the quilting process, you may prefer to cut 6" (15.2cm) both wider and longer than your finished project dimensions. Trim after quilting.

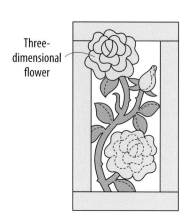

Three-dimensional flower

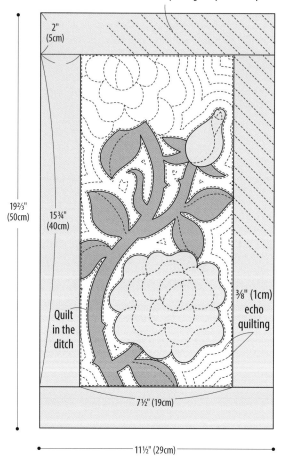

Make sure the quilting adapts to the pattern.

2" (5cm)

19⅔" (50cm)

15¾" (40cm)

⅜" (1cm) echo quilting

Quilt in the ditch

7½" (19cm)

11½" (29cm)

3D Flower Petals (one piece each)

How to Construct the 3D Flower

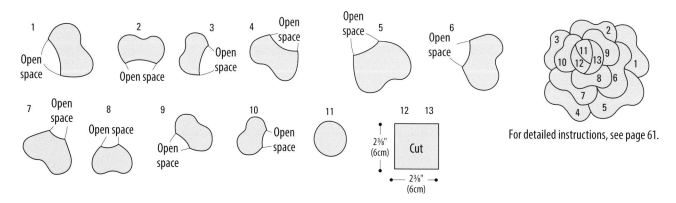

For detailed instructions, see page 61.

Instructions

1) Take care of the appliqué and the border. Complete the top section.
2) Sandwich the top over the cotton batting and the backing, tack them, leave border, and start quilting.
3) Cut the cotton batting as needed, fold the top back, and wrap it up.
4) Fold the backing's seam allowance and blindstitch it to the folded-back top.
5) Quilt the border.
6) Construct the three-dimensional flower and then sew it onto the quilt.

Instructions

Photocopy at 200%

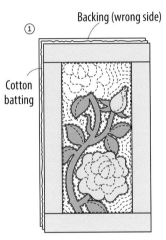

Create the main body. For more detailed instructions, see pages 108 and 109. Only quilt the inner section, leaving the border.

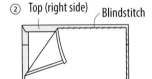

Cut the cotton batting as needed. Fold the top's seam allowance. Also fold the backing's seam allowance. Then sew them onto the folded-back top.

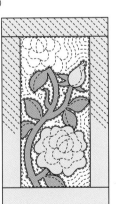

Quilt the fabric parts on the border.

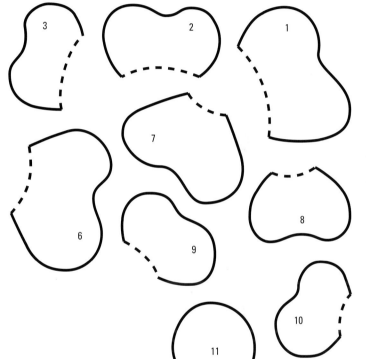

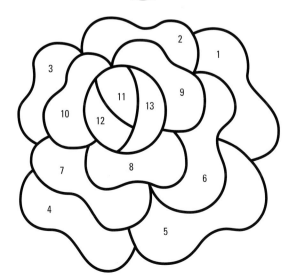

Materials

Main body B fabric (includes main body A fabric):
   27½" x 27½" (70 x 70cm)
Motif fabric A: 15¾" x 23⅔" (40 x 60cm)
Cotton batting: 27½" x 27½" (70 x 70cm)*
Backing fabric: 27½" x 27½" (70 x 70cm)*

Lining fabric (includes pocket): 31½" x 31½" (80 x 80cm)
Piping cord fabric: 15¾" x 19⅔" (40 x 50cm)
Store-bought handle: 33½" x 1½" (85 x 4cm)
Thick embroidery thread: as needed
Piping cord: as needed

* Note: To ensure your backing and batting remain large enough to accommodate the quilt front following the quilting process, you may prefer to cut 6" (15.2cm) both wider and longer than your finished project dimensions. Trim after quilting.

Main Body (two pieces)

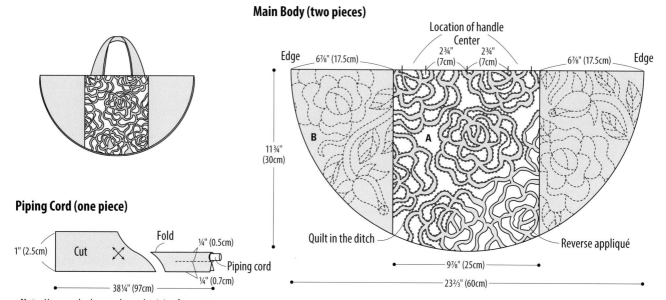

Piping Cord (one piece)

Note: You can also buy ready-made piping from a store.

Lining (two pieces)

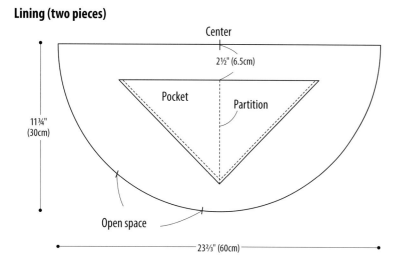

Pocket (one piece)

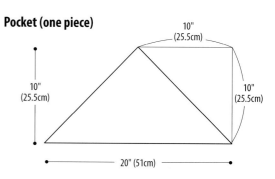

How to Make the Pocket

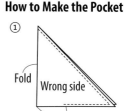

① Fold it by the middle and sew all around, leaving an open space.

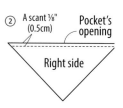

② Turn right side out, arrange the open space's seam allowance, then stitch the pocket's opening.

Instructions

1) Take care of the reverse appliqué, join A and B, and complete the main body's top section.
2) Sandwich the top over the cotton batting and the backing, tack them, and start quilting.
3) Create the piping cord. Sew it around the entire body with a sewing machine.
4) Unite the two pieces of the main body and sew them together around the edges.
5) Create the pocket, attach it to the lining, then sew the lining.
6) Temporarily attach the handle to the main body, fold the lining on itself, and sew it at the bag opening.
7) Turn right side out, close the open space, and keep the lining in place with a cover stitch.

How to Attach the Handle

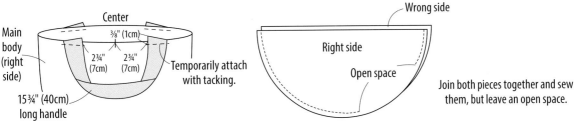

Center
⅜" (1cm)
Main body (right side)
2¾" (7cm)   2¾" (7cm)
Temporarily attach with tacking.
15¾" (40cm) long handle

Join it diagonally against the mouth of the main body and sew it. To make your own handle, see page 99.

How to Make the Lining

Wrong side
Right side
Open space

Join both pieces together and sew them, but leave an open space.

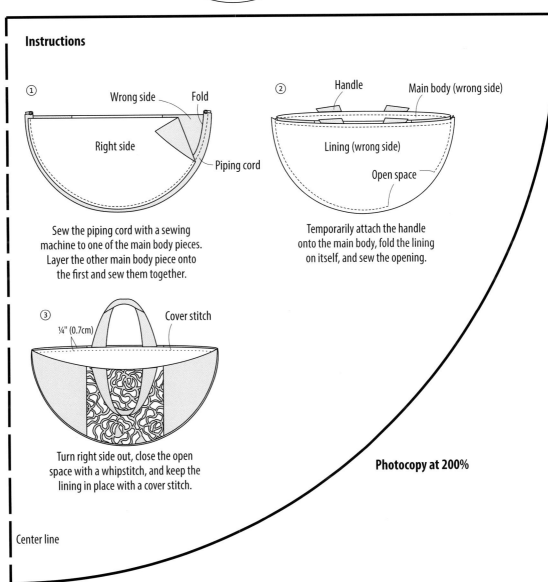

Instructions

① Wrong side   Fold
Right side
Piping cord

Sew the piping cord with a sewing machine to one of the main body pieces. Layer the other main body piece onto the first and sew them together.

② Handle   Main body (wrong side)
Lining (wrong side)
Open space

Temporarily attach the handle onto the main body, fold the lining on itself, and sew the opening.

③ ¼" (0.7cm)   Cover stitch

Turn right side out, close the open space with a whipstitch, and keep the lining in place with a cover stitch.

Center line

Photocopy at 200%

Materials

Body fabric (includes exterior bottom, interior lid, base fabric for
  exterior lid, binding, and supplementary fabric):
  13¾" x 39⅜" (35 x 100cm)
Motif fabric (for exterior lid): 5⅞" x 7⅞" (15 x 20cm)
Backing fabric: 11¾" x 21⅔" (30 x 55cm)
Cotton batting: 11¾" x 37⅜" (30 x 95cm)
Lining (for body, includes interior bottom): 7⅞" x 27½" (20 x 70cm)

Piping cord fabric: 13¾" x 13¾" (35 x 35cm)
Thick fusible web: 4" x 19⅔" (10 x 50cm)
Zipper: 8" (20cm)
Plastic insert: 5⅞" x 5⅞" (15 x 15cm)
Thick embroidery thread: as needed
Piping cord: as needed

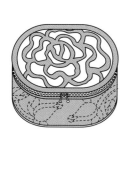

Exterior Lid (one piece)

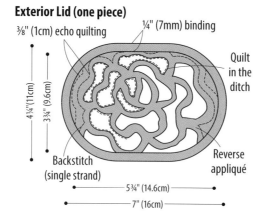

⅜" (1cm) echo quilting
¼" (7mm) binding
Quilt in the ditch
Backstitch (single strand)
Reverse appliqué
4¼" (11cm)
3¾" (9.6cm)
5¾" (14.6cm)
7" (16cm)

Interior Lid (one piece)

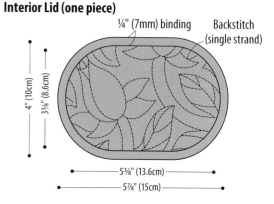

¼" (7mm) binding
Backstitch (single strand)
4" (10cm)
3⅜" (8.6cm)
5⅜" (13.6cm)
5⅞" (15cm)

Piping Cord (one piece)

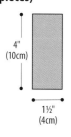

1" (2.5cm)
Cut
Fold
¼" (0.5cm)
¼" (0.7cm)
Piping cord
18½" (47cm)

Note: You can also buy ready-made piping from a store.

Exterior Bottom (one piece)

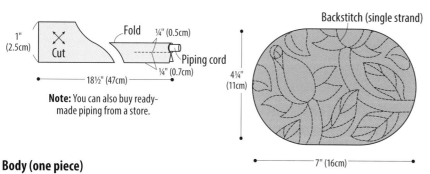

Backstitch (single strand)
4¼" (11cm)
7" (16cm)

Interior Bottom, Quilt Cotton, & Plastic Insert (one piece each)

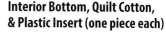

4" (10cm)
5⅞" (15cm)

Note: The cotton batting and the plastic insert need to be cut. Also, leave 1⅓" (3.5cm) of seam allowance on the bottom.

Body (one piece)

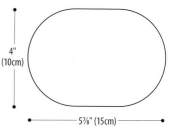

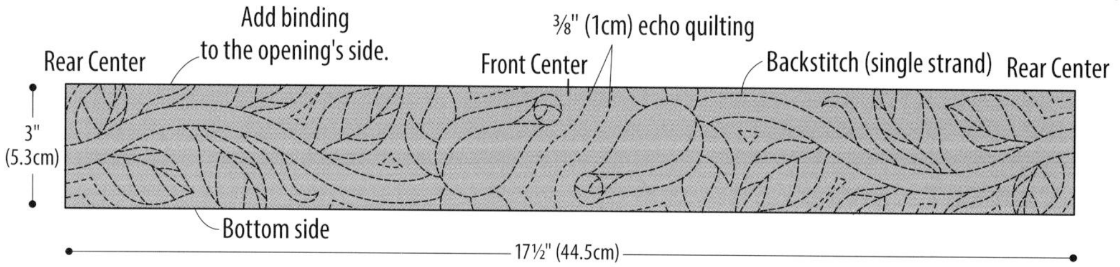

Rear Center
Add binding to the opening's side.
Front Center
⅜" (1cm) echo quilting
Backstitch (single strand)
Rear Center
3" (5.3cm)
Bottom side
17½" (44.5cm)

Note: After embroidering, stick some thick fusible web onto the backing's cut.

Lining (one piece)

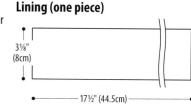

3⅛" (8cm)
17½" (44.5cm)

Supplementary Fabrics (two pieces)

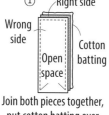

4" (10cm)
1½" (4cm)

How to Create the Supplementary Fabric

① Right side
Wrong side
Cotton batting
Open space

② Right side

Join both pieces together, put cotton batting over them, sew all around it, and leave an open space.

Turn right side out and seal the open space.

How to Make the Interior Bottom

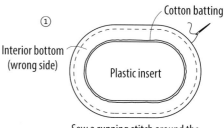

Cotton batting
① Interior bottom (wrong side)
Plastic insert

Sew a running stitch around the fabric's edges and layer the cotton batting with the plastic insert.

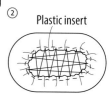

② Plastic insert

Pull the running stitch tight and sew a thread through it to keep it in place.

Instructions

1) Take care of the reverse appliqué and complete the exterior lid. The body, interior lid, and exterior bottom's tops are one piece of fabric.
2) Sandwich the top over the cotton batting and the backing, tack them, and start to quilt and embroider.
3) Use binding to seal the edges of the exterior lid and the interior lid.
4) Sew the body into a circle. Create piping cord and use a sewing machine to sew it to the bottom of the body.

How to Make the Main Body

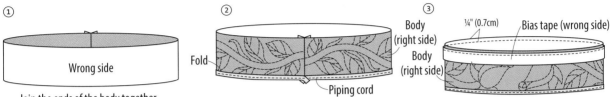

① Join the ends of the body together in a ring and sew them. Sew the lining in the same way.

② Sew piping cord to the body's bottom side with a sewing machine.

③ Place bias tape, folded into a ring, over the side opening. Sew it. Don't use two layers of bias tape; just do a single binding with one layer.

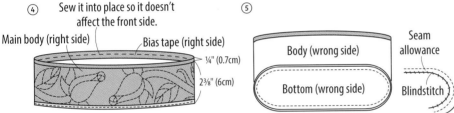

④ Turn the bias tape into the lining and sew it all, leaving the seam allowance extended.

⑤ Join the main body and the bottom together and sew them. Let the seam allowance drop onto the bottom and blindstitch it.

Instructions

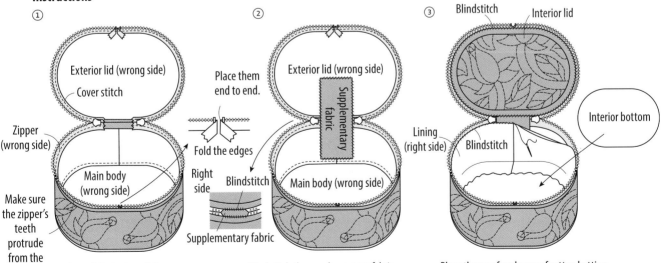

① Spread the body and the lid to the left and right. Sew two zippers on. Make sure the zipper's teeth protrude from the binding.

② Blindstitch the supplementary fabric to the base of the zippers. Blindstitch and bind the supplementary fabric to the exterior lid and the back of the main body (as shown).

③ Place three or four layers of cotton batting over the exterior lid's wrong side to puff it up a little, then blindstitch the interior lid. Insert the lining in the main body, fold its seam allowance, and blindstitch it to the zipper. Insert the interior bottom and sew it into place.

See pattern on page 122

Materials

Base fabric: 43¼" x 43¼" (110 x 110cm)
Motif fabric A (navy blue): 23⅝" x 31½" (60 x 80cm)
Motif fabric B (blue): 29½" x 43¼" (75 x 110cm)
Cotton batting: 43¼" x 43¼" (110 x 110cm)*
Backing fabric: 43¼" x 43¼" (110 x 110cm)*
Binding fabric: 39¼" x 43¼" (100 x 110cm)
Thick embroidery thread: as needed

Instructions

1) Place the base fabric over motif fabric A. Create the sperm whale with reverse appliqué.
2) Place the results of step 1 onto motif fabric B. Do more reverse appliqué to finish the top section.
3) Place the top onto the cotton batting and the backing, tack it, and begin embroidering and quilting.
4) Keep the border contained with double binding.

* Note: To ensure your backing and batting remain large enough to accommodate the quilt front following the quilting process, you may prefer to cut 10" (25.4cm) both wider and longer than your finished project dimensions. Trim after quilting.

How to Sew the Satin Stitch

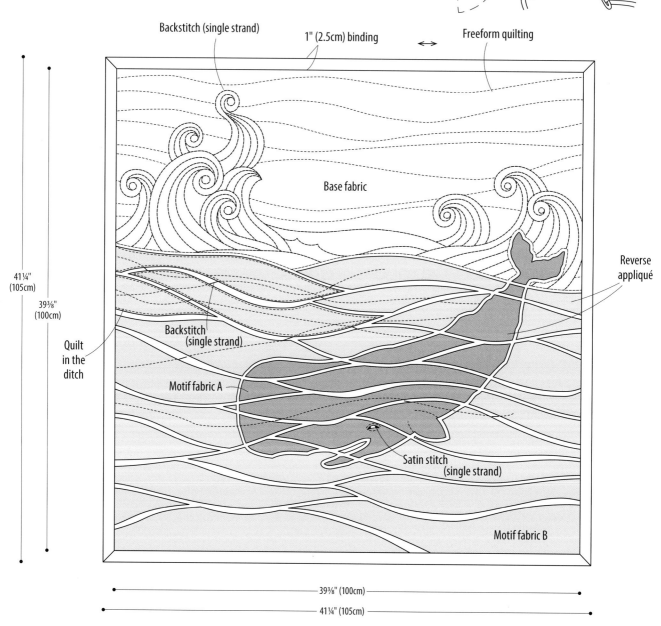

The sperm whale part and the white waves are a backstitch that continues from the quilting.

Materials

Base fabric: 9⅞" x 13¾"
(25 x 35cm)

Appliqué fabric: 7⅞" x 11¾"
(20 x 30cm)

Main body fabric (for back):
9⅞" x 13¾" (25 x 35cm)

Cotton batting: 9⅞" x 27½"
(25 x 70cm)

Backing fabric: 9⅞" x 27½"
(25 x 70cm)

Lining fabric: 9⅞" x 27½"
(25 x 70cm)

Piping cord fabric: 11¾" x 11¾"
(30 x 30cm)

Zipper: 11¾" (30cm)

Thick embroidery thread:
as needed

Piping cord: as needed

Instructions

1) Take care of the appliqué and complete the top section for the front of the main body. The back of the main body is one piece.

2) Sandwich the top over the cotton batting and the backing, tack them, and start to quilt and embroider.

3) Create your piping cord and sew it onto the edges of the main body with a sewing machine.

4) Fold the main body's front and back. Sew them. Sew the lining in the same way.

5) Attach the zipper to the main body's opening. Insert the lining and blindstitch it.

Front of Main Body (one piece)

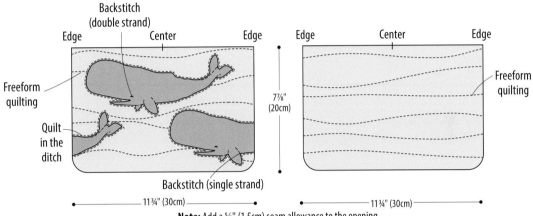

Backstitch (double strand)

Edge · Center · Edge

Freeform quilting

Quilt in the ditch

Backstitch (single strand)

⊢ 11¾" (30cm) ⊣

Back of Main Body (one piece)

Edge · Center · Edge

7⅞" (20cm)

Freeform quilting

⊢ 11¾" (30cm) ⊣

Note: Add a ⅝" (1.5cm) seam allowance to the opening.

Lining (two pieces)

Edge · Center · Edge

7⅞" (20cm)

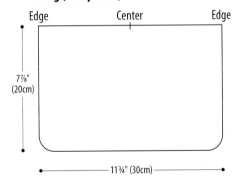

⊢ 11¾" (30cm) ⊣

Piping Cord (one piece)

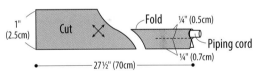

1" (2.5cm)

Cut

Fold

¼" (0.5cm)

Piping cord

¼" (0.7cm)

⊢ 27½" (70cm) ⊣

Note: You can also buy ready-made piping from a store.

Instructions

①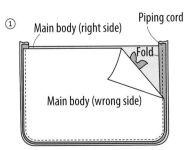

Main body (right side)

Piping cord

Fold

Main body (wrong side)

Sew piping cord onto the main body's front with a sewing machine. Fold it over the main body's back and sew around the edges.

②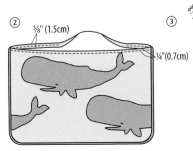

⅝" (1.5cm)

¼" (0.7cm)

Turn right side out, fold the opening's seam allowance, and finally sew it.

③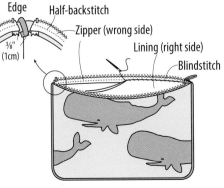

Edge — Half-backstitch

Zipper (wrong side)

Lining (right side)

Blindstitch

⅜" (1cm)

Place the zipper onto the main body's opening so the zipper's teeth show. Sew it in place with a half-backstitch. Insert the lining and blindstitch it.

Materials

Main body fabric A: 13¾" x 35⅜" (35 x 90cm)

Main body fabric B: 13¾" x 19¾" (35 x 50cm)

Appliqué fabric: 11¾" x 35⅜" (30 x 90cm)

Cotton batting: 27½" x 27½" (70 x 70cm)*

Backing fabric: 27½" x 27½" (70 x 70cm)*

Lining fabric (includes pocket): 39⅜" x 27½" (100 x 70cm)

Piping cord fabric: 15¾" x 19⅔" (40 x 50cm)

Store-bought handle: 33½" x 1½" (85 x 4cm)

Thick embroidery thread: as needed

Piping cord: as needed

* Note: To ensure your backing and batting remain large enough to accommodate the quilt front following the quilting process, you may prefer to cut 6" (15.2cm) both wider and longer than your finished project dimensions. Trim after quilting.

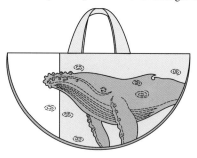

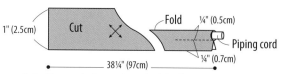

Piping Cord (one piece)

1" (2.5cm) — Cut

Fold — ¼" (0.5cm) — Piping cord

¼" (0.7cm)

38¼" (97cm)

Note: You can also buy ready-made piping from a store.

Front of Main Body (one piece)

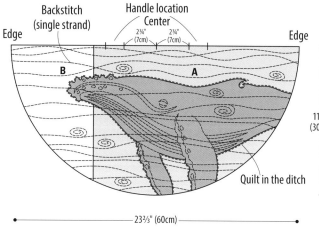

Backstitch (single strand)

Handle location / Center

2¾" (7cm)   2¾" (7cm)

Edge — B — A — Edge

Quilt in the ditch

23⅔" (60cm)

11¾" (30cm)

Back of Main Body (one piece)

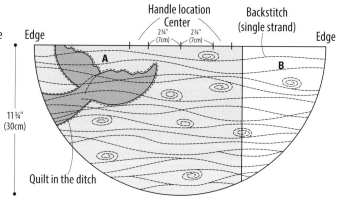

Handle location / Center

2¾" (7cm)   2¾" (7cm)

Backstitch (single strand)

Edge — A — B — Edge

Quilt in the ditch

23⅔" (60cm)

Lining (two pieces)

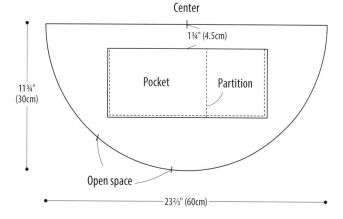

Center

1¾" (4.5cm)

Pocket   Partition

11¾" (30cm)

Open space

23⅔" (60cm)

Pocket (one piece)

11¾" (30cm)

11¾" (30cm)

How to Make the Pocket

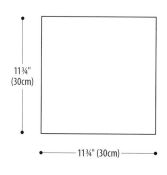

① Fold

Open space

Wrong side

Fold at the middle and sew around the edges, leaving an open space.

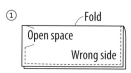

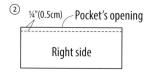

② ¼" (0.5cm) — Pocket's opening

Right side

Turn right side out. Seal the open space in the seam allowance and stitch the pocket's opening.

Instructions

1) Join fabrics A and B together. Take care of the main body's appliqué and complete its top.
2) Sandwich the top over the cotton batting and the backing. Tack them and start quilting as well as embroidering.
3) Create some piping cord and use a sewing machine to attach it to the edges of the main body.
4) Join both main body pieces together and sew their edges.
5) Create the pocket and sew it to the lining.
6) Temporarily attach the handle to the main body. Join the lining to the body and sew the opening.
7) Turn right side out, close the open space, and seal it with a cover stitch.

How to Attach the Handle

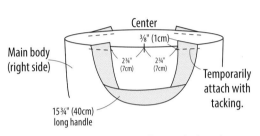

Join it diagonally against the main body and sew it. To make your own handle, see page 99.

How to Make the Lining

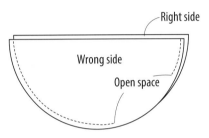

Join both pieces to each other and sew around the edges, leaving an open space.

Instructions

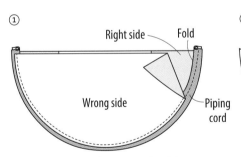

① Use a sewing machine to sew the piping cord onto one piece of the main body. Join the other piece of the main body to the first one and sew them.

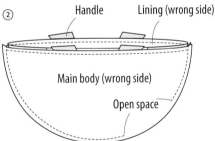

② Temporarily attach the handle to the main body, fold the lining on itself, and sew its opening.

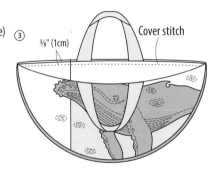

③ Turn right side out, close the open space with a whipstitch, and keep the lining in place with a cover stitch.

See pattern on page 123

Materials

Base fabric: 15¾" x 23⅔" (40 x 60cm)
Appliqué fabric (includes gusset): 15¾" x 39⅜" (40 x 100cm)
Cotton batting: 15¾" x 39⅜" (40 x 100cm)
Backing fabric: 15¾" x 39⅜" (40 x 100cm)
Lining fabric (includes pocket): 33½" x 21⅔" (85 x 55cm)

Piping cord fabric: 15¾" x 23⅔" (40 x 60cm)
Store-bought handle: 29½" x 1½" (75 x 4cm)
Thick embroidery thread: as needed
Piping cord: as needed

Gusset (one piece)

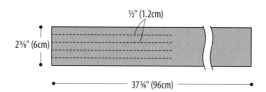

½" (1.2cm)
2⅜" (6cm)
37¾" (96cm)

Piping Cord (two pieces)

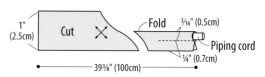

1" (2.5cm)
Cut
Fold
3/16" (0.5cm)
Piping cord
¼" (0.7cm)
39⅜" (100cm)

Note: You can also buy ready-made piping from a store.

Main Body (two pieces)

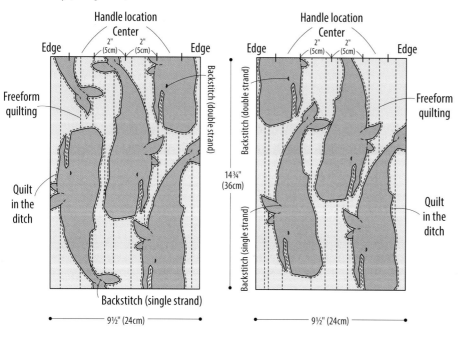

Handle location
Center
Edge   2" (5cm)   2" (5cm)   Edge
Freeform quilting
Backstitch (double strand)
Quilt in the ditch
Backstitch (single strand)
9½" (24cm)

Handle location
Center
Edge   2" (5cm)   2" (5cm)   Edge
Freeform quilting
Backstitch (double strand)
14¾" (36cm)
Quilt in the ditch
Backstitch (single strand)
9½" (24cm)

Lining (one piece)

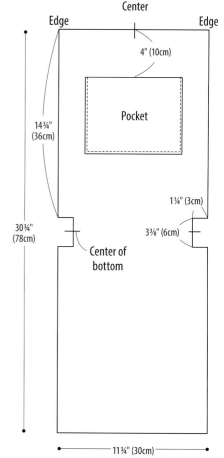

Edge   Center   Edge
4" (10cm)
Pocket
14¾" (36cm)
1¼" (3cm)
3⅜" (6cm)
30¾" (78cm)
Center of bottom
11¾" (30cm)

Pocket (one piece)

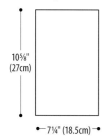

10⅝" (27cm)
7¼" (18.5cm)

How to Make the Pocket

① Open space
Wrong side
Fold

Fold it in half and sew the edges, leaving an open space.

② Right side

Turn right side out. Fold the open space's seam allowance under and close it with stitches.

Instructions

1) Take care of the appliqué and complete the top section. The gusset's top is one piece.
2) Sandwich the top over the cotton batting and the backing. Tack them and start quilting as well as embroidering.
3) Create your piping cord. Sew it onto both edges of the gusset with a sewing machine.
4) Create the pocket and attach it to the lining. Sew the lining.
5) Join the main body and the gusset's bottom. Sew them together.
6) Join the main body and the gusset's edges. Sew them together.
7) Temporarily attach the handle to the main body, fold the lining together, and sew it.
8) Turn right side out, close the bag opening, and keep the lining in place with a cover stitch.

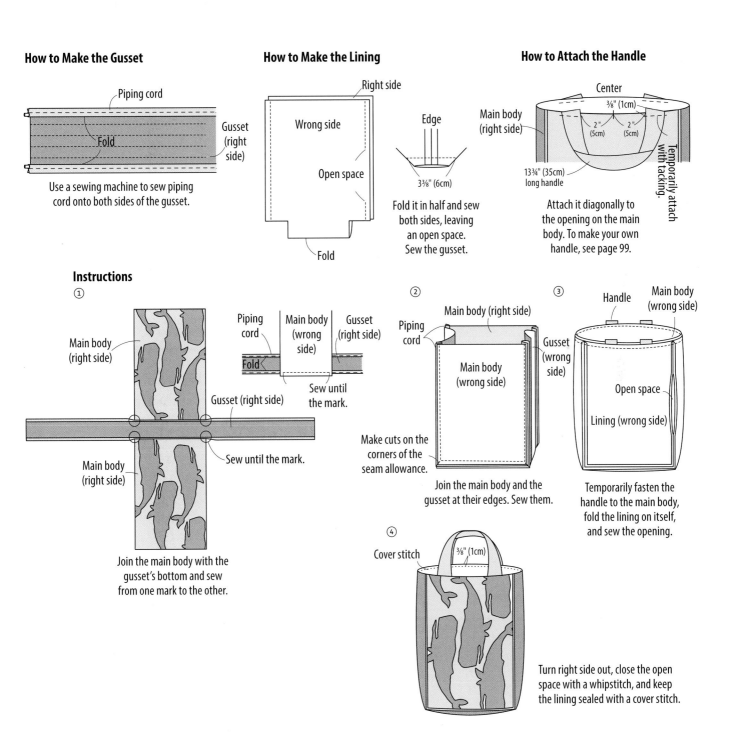

How to Make the Gusset

Piping cord

Fold

Gusset (right side)

Use a sewing machine to sew piping cord onto both sides of the gusset.

How to Make the Lining

Right side

Wrong side

Open space

Fold

Edge

3⅜" (6cm)

Fold it in half and sew both sides, leaving an open space. Sew the gusset.

How to Attach the Handle

Center

⅜" (1cm)

Main body (right side)

2" (5cm) 2" (5cm)

13¾" (35cm) long handle

Temporarily attach with tacking.

Attach it diagonally to the opening on the main body. To make your own handle, see page 99.

Instructions

①

Main body (right side)

Gusset (right side)

Main body (right side)

Piping cord

Fold

Main body (wrong side)

Gusset (right side)

Sew until the mark.

Sew until the mark.

Join the main body with the gusset's bottom and sew from one mark to the other.

②

Main body (right side)

Piping cord

Main body (wrong side)

Gusset (wrong side)

Make cuts on the corners of the seam allowance.

Join the main body and the gusset at their edges. Sew them.

③

Handle

Main body (wrong side)

Open space

Lining (wrong side)

Temporarily fasten the handle to the main body, fold the lining on itself, and sew the opening.

④

Cover stitch

⅜" (1cm)

Turn right side out, close the open space with a whipstitch, and keep the lining sealed with a cover stitch.

Small Manta Ray Bag & Small Green Sea Turtle Bag See pattern on page 124

Materials

Base fabric: 13¾" x 13¾" (35 x 35cm)

Appliqué fabric: 11¾" x 11¾" (30 x 30cm)

Main body fabric (for back): 13¾" x 13¾" (35 x 35cm)

Cotton batting: 27½" x 13¾" (70 x 35cm)

Backing fabric: 27½" x 13¾" (70 x 35cm)

Lining fabric: 27½" x 13¾" (70 x 35cm)

Piping cord fabric: 11¾" x 11¾" (30 x 30cm)

Store-bought handle: 21⅔" x 1½" (55 x 4cm)

Sewable magnet button: ⁹⁄₁₆" (1.4cm) diameter

Thick embroidery thread: as needed

Piping cord: as needed

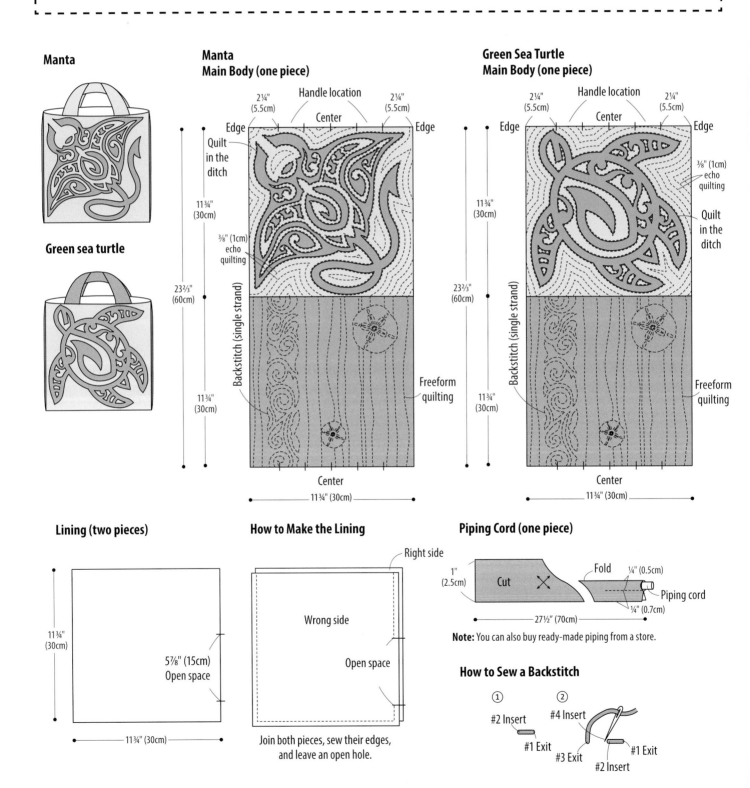

Note: You can also buy ready-made piping from a store.

Join both pieces, sew their edges, and leave an open hole.

Instructions

1) Take care of the appliqué, join the main body's front and back, and then complete the top section of the main body.
2) Sandwich the top over the cotton batting and the backing, tack them and start quilting as well as embroidering.
3) Create some piping cord and use a sewing machine to attach it to the edges of the main body.
4) Fold the main body in two and sew the joint edges.
5) Sew the lining, leaving an open space.
6) Temporarily attach the handle to the main body, then join the inside of the bag to the outer body and sew the opening.
7) Turn right side out, close the open space and seal it with a cover stitch.
8) Sew the magnet button on.

Handle (two pieces)

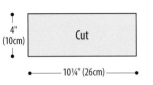

4" (10cm)

Cut

10¼" (26cm)

How to Make the Handle

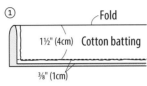

① Fold

1½" (4cm)   Cotton batting

⅜" (1cm)

Fold in half, add a layer of cotton batting, and sew it.

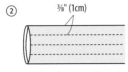

② ⅜" (1cm)

Turn right side out and stitch it.

How to Attach the Handle

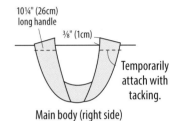

10¼" (26cm) long handle

⅜" (1cm)

Temporarily attach with tacking.

Main body (right side)

Attach it diagonally to the opening on the main body.

Instructions

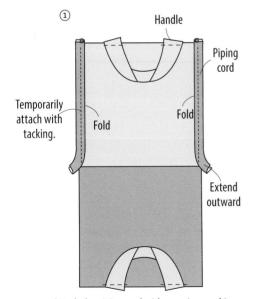

① Handle

Piping cord

Temporarily attach with tacking.

Fold

Fold

Extend outward

Attach the piping cord with a sewing machine. Temporarily attach the handle with tacking.

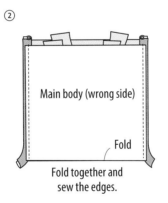

②

Main body (wrong side)

Fold

Fold together and sew the edges.

③ Main body (wrong side)   Handle

Lining (wrong side)

Open space

Insert the lining into the main body and sew the opening.

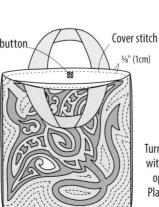

④ Magnet button   Cover stitch

⅜" (1cm)

Turn right side out, close the open space with a whipstitch, and keep the lining's opening in place with a cover stitch. Place the magnet button in the center.

Materials

Base piecing fabric: fabric scraps at least 7⅞" (20cm) long and ³⁄₁₆" to ¾" (5 to 20mm) wide (as needed)

Motif appliqué fabric: 7⅞" x 9⅞" (20 x 25cm)

Cotton batting: 13¾" x 19⅔" (35 x 50cm)

Backing fabric: 13¾" x 19⅔" (35 x 50cm)

Lining fabric: 13¾" x 19⅔" (35 x 50cm)

Fish-shaped button: 1¾" (4.5cm) long

Piping cord fabric: 11¾" x 11¾" (30 x 30cm)

Piping cord: as needed

Instructions

1) Sandwich the cotton batting and the backing together and take care of the appliqué on the base fabric.
2) Take care of the motif's appliqué and embroider it.
3) Create piping cord and sew it around the edges of the main body.
4) Join the main body together and sew its edges.
5) Sew the lining, leaving an open space.
6) Join the main body and the lining. Sew the bag opening.
7) Turn right side out, close the open space, then keep the lining contained with a cover stitch.
8) Add the button.

Main Body (two pieces)

Lining (two pieces)

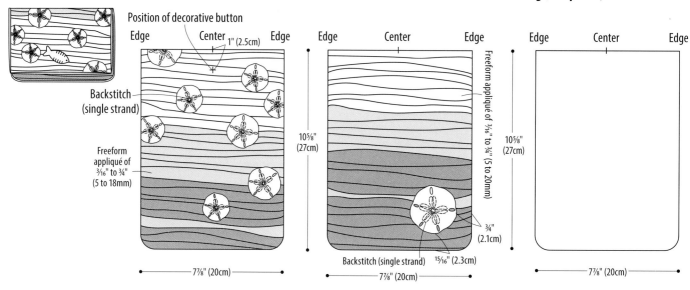

How to Make the Main Body's Base

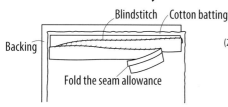

Cut pieces of cloth ¼" to ¾" (5 to 20mm) wide. Sandwich them in order, blindstitching each to the cloth below it.

How to Make the Lining

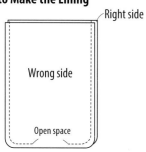

Join both pieces onto each other and sew around the edges, leaving an open space.

Piping Cord (one piece)

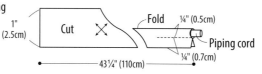

Note: You can also buy ready-made piping from a store.

Instructions

①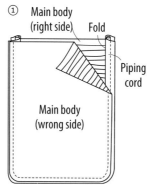

Sew the piping cord with a sewing machine to one of the main body pieces. Layer the other main body piece onto the first and sew them together.

②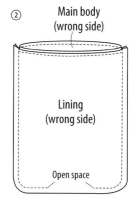

Join the main body and the lining. Sew the opening.

③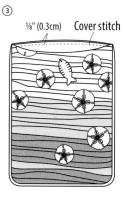

Turn right side out, close the open space with a whipstitch, and keep the lining in place with a cover stitch.

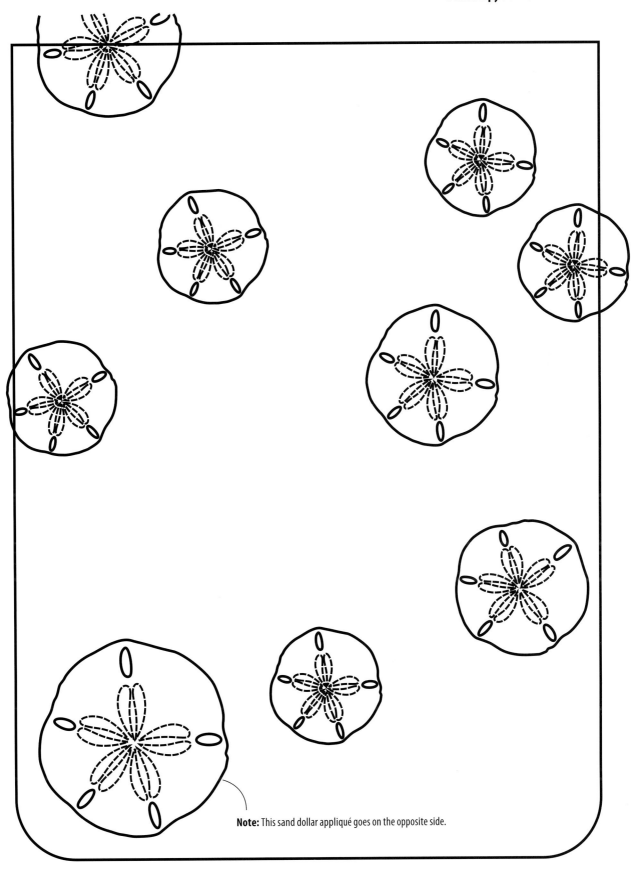

Note: This sand dollar appliqué goes on the opposite side.

Materials

Main body fabric (includes facing): 43¼" x 17¾" (110 x 45cm)
Lining fabric (includes pocket): 43¼" x 17¾" (110 x 45cm)
Fusible web: 43¼" x 17¾" (110 x 45cm)
Leather strap (for handle): 27½" x 1½" (70 x 4cm)
Plastic insert: 7⅞" x 9⅞" (20 x 25cm)
Thick embroidery thread: as needed

Instructions

1) Embroider the main body and stick fusible web to the wrong side.
2) Fold the main body in two, then sew both edges as well as the gusset.
3) Create the pocket, attach it to the lining, and sew the lining.
4) Temporarily attach the handle to the main body, fold the lining on itself, and sew the opening.
5) Turn right side out, insert the plastic insert, close the open space, and keep the opening area contained with stitching.

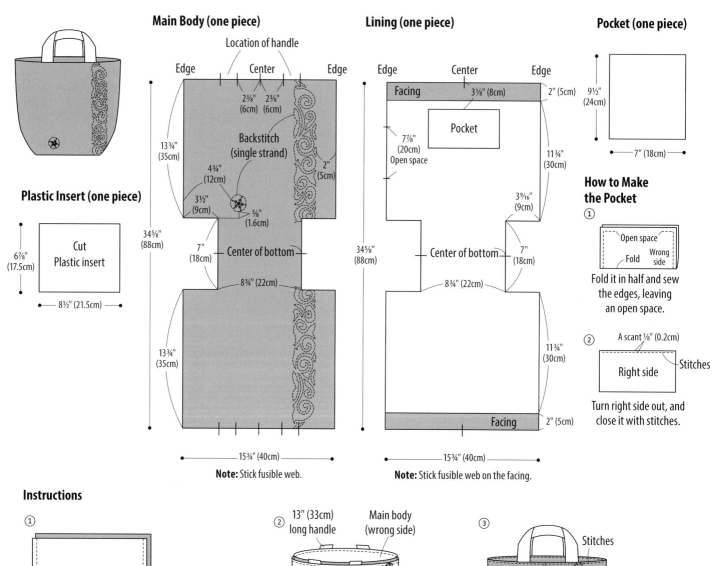

Main Body (one piece)
Location of handle
Edge — Center — Edge
2⅜" (6cm) 2⅜" (6cm)
Backstitch (single strand)
4¾" (12cm)
3½" (9cm)
⅝" (1.6cm)
13¾" (35cm)
2" (5cm)
34⅝" (88cm)
7" (18cm)
Center of bottom
8¾" (22cm)
13¾" (35cm)
15¾" (40cm)
Note: Stick fusible web.

Lining (one piece)
Edge — Center — Edge
Facing 3⅛" (8cm) 2" (5cm)
Pocket
7⅞" (20cm) Open space
11¾" (30cm)
3⁹⁄₁₆" (9cm)
34⅝" (88cm)
Center of bottom
7" (18cm)
8¾" (22cm)
11¾" (30cm)
Facing 2" (5cm)
15¾" (40cm)
Note: Stick fusible web on the facing.

Pocket (one piece)
9½" (24cm)
7" (18cm)

Plastic Insert (one piece)
Cut
Plastic insert
6⅞" (17.5cm)
8½" (21.5cm)

How to Make the Pocket
① Open space
Fold Wrong side
Fold it in half and sew the edges, leaving an open space.
② A scant ⅛" (0.2cm)
Right side Stitches
Turn right side out, and close it with stitches.

Instructions

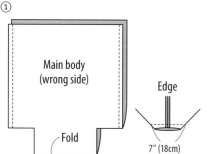

① Main body (wrong side)
Fold
Edge
7" (18cm)

Fold it in half. Sew both edges and the gusset. Sew the lining's edges in the same way, but leave an open space.

② 13" (33cm) long handle   Main body (wrong side)
Lining (wrong side)

Temporarily attach the handle to the main body's opening. Fold the lining and sew its opening.

③ Stitches
⅛" (0.3cm)

Turn right side out, insert the plastic insert, seal the open space with a whipstitch, and topstitch around the bag opening.

Photocopy at 100%

To create a continuous pattern, overlap the shapes at the circled locations.

31, 32, & 33 Pouches with L-Shaped Zipper

See pattern on page 124

Materials

Base fabric: 9⅞" x 9⅞" (25 x 25cm)
Appliqué fabric: 9⅞" x 9⅞" (25 x 25cm)
Cotton batting: 9⅞" x 9⅞" (25 x 25cm)
Backing fabric: 9⅞" x 9⅞" (25 x 25cm)
Lining fabric: 9⅞" x 9⅞" (25 x 25cm)
Thick fusible web: 7⅞" x 7⅞" (20 x 20cm)
Zipper: 11¾" (30cm)

Instructions

1) Take care of the appliqué and complete the top section of the main body.
2) Sandwich the top over the cotton batting and the backing, tack them, and start quilting.
3) Stick a cut of thick fusible web onto the wrong side.
4) Fold in half and sew the edges.
5) Sew the lining in the exact same way as the main body.
6) Fold the seam allowance of the main body's opening and then sew the zipper.
7) Insert the lining into the main body. Blindstitch it to the zipper.

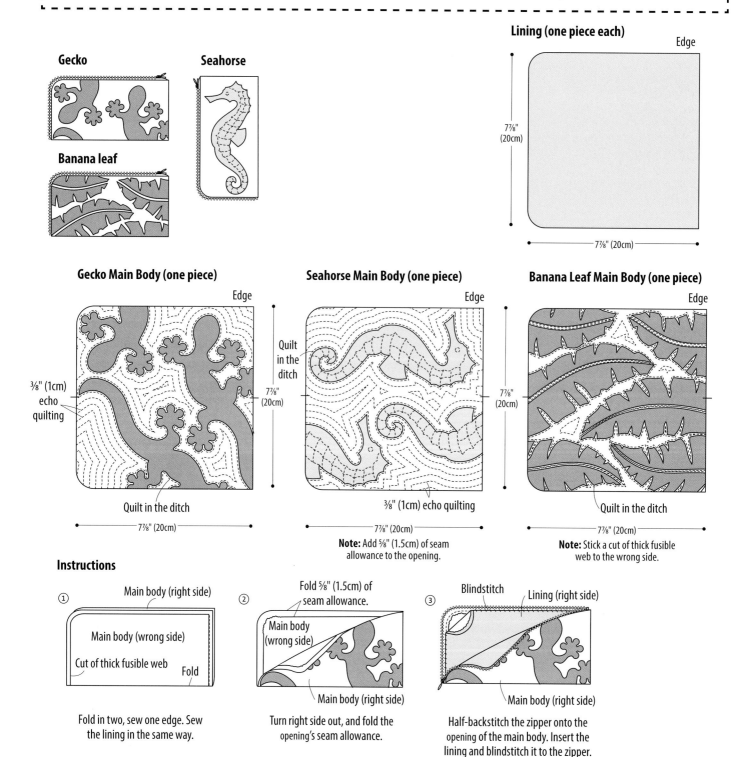

Gecko

Seahorse

Banana leaf

Lining (one piece each)

Edge

7⅞" (20cm)

7⅞" (20cm)

Gecko Main Body (one piece)

Edge

⅜" (1cm) echo quilting

Quilt in the ditch

7⅞" (20cm)

7⅞" (20cm)

Seahorse Main Body (one piece)

Edge

Quilt in the ditch

⅜" (1cm) echo quilting

7⅞" (20cm)

7⅞" (20cm)

Note: Add ⅝" (1.5cm) of seam allowance to the opening.

Banana Leaf Main Body (one piece)

Edge

Quilt in the ditch

7⅞" (20cm)

7⅞" (20cm)

Note: Stick a cut of thick fusible web to the wrong side.

Instructions

① Main body (right side)
Main body (wrong side)
Cut of thick fusible web
Fold

Fold in two, sew one edge. Sew the lining in the same way.

② Fold ⅝" (1.5cm) of seam allowance.
Main body (wrong side)
Main body (right side)

Turn right side out, and fold the opening's seam allowance.

③ Blindstitch   Lining (right side)
Main body (right side)

Half-backstitch the zipper onto the opening of the main body. Insert the lining and blindstitch it to the zipper.

Materials

Appliqué fabric: fabric scraps (as needed)

Leaves appliqué fabric: fabric scraps (as needed)

Flowers appliqué fabric: fabric scraps (as needed)

Border fabric: 15¾" x 17¾" (40 x 45cm)

Cotton batting: 19⅔" x 19⅔" (50 x 50cm)

Backing fabric: 19⅔" x 19⅔" (50 x 50cm)

33 beads: ⁵/₃₂" (4mm) diameter

Thick fusible web: as needed

Instructions

1) Sandwich the cotton batting and the backing, take care of the appliqué, and complete the central section.

2) Create the border. Layer it over the wrong side of the center created in step 1 and sew its edges.

3) Turn the border right side out, and blindstitch it to the central section.

4) Take care of the palm tree appliqué and sew the bougainvillea on.

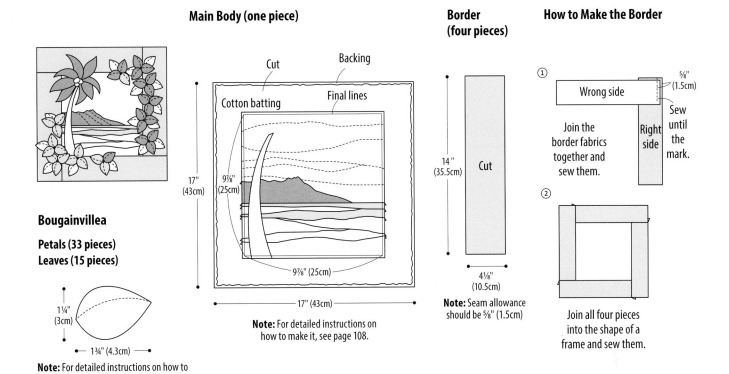

Main Body (one piece)

Border (four pieces)

How to Make the Border

① Join the border fabrics together and sew them. Sew until the mark. ⅝" (1.5cm)

② Join all four pieces into the shape of a frame and sew them.

Note: For detailed instructions on how to make it, see page 108.

Note: Seam allowance should be ⅝" (1.5cm)

Bougainvillea

Petals (33 pieces)
Leaves (15 pieces)

1¼" (3cm) 1¾" (4.3cm)

Note: For detailed instructions on how to make them, see pages 61, 107, and 109.

Finishing Touches

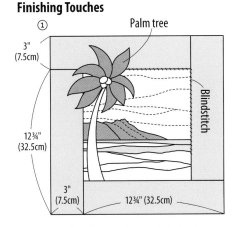

Sew the main body and the border together. Attach the palm tree leaves and fruits as appliqué. For more detailed instructions, see pages 108–109.

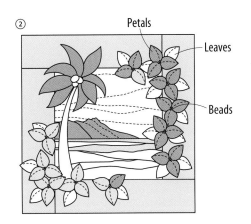

Sew the leaves, petals, and beads of the bougainvillea in place.

Photocopy at 100%

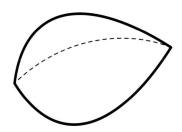

Materials

Appliqué fabric: fabric scraps (as needed)

Palm trees appliqué fabric: 13¾" x 17¾" (35 x 45cm)

Sky appliqué fabric: 11¾" x 17¾" (30 x 45cm)

Petals appliqué fabric: 19⅔" x 11¾" (50 x 30cm)

Leaves appliqué fabric (two types): 19⅔" x 7⅞" (50 x 20cm) each

Border fabric: 15¾" x 23⅔" (40 x 60cm)

Cotton batting: 19⅔" x 23⅔" (50 x 60cm)

Backing fabric: 19⅔" x 23⅔" (50 x 60cm)

Thick embroidery thread: as needed

Thick fusible web: as needed

Main Body (one piece)

Quilt in the ditch

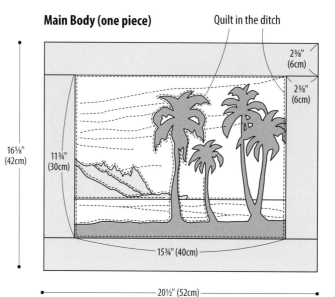

2⅜" (6cm)

2⅜" (6cm)

16⅝" (42cm)

11¾" (30cm)

15¾" (40cm)

20½" (52cm)

Petals (25 pieces)

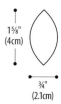

1⅝" (4cm)

¾" (2.1cm)

Note: For detailed instructions on how to make them, see pages 61, 107, and 109.

Leaves (15 pieces)

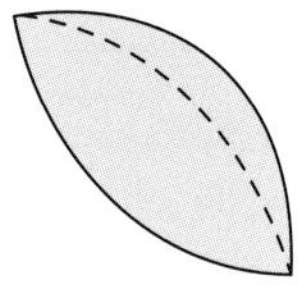

Cut them in proportion to the pattern paper.

Note: For detailed instructions on how to make them, see pages 61, 107, and 109.

How to Make the Main Body

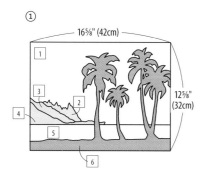

① 16⅝" (42cm)

12⅝" (32cm)

Complete the central section appliqués in the order given.

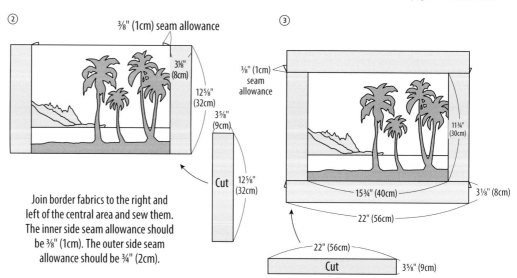

② ⅜" (1cm) seam allowance

3⅛" (8cm)

12⅝" (32cm)

3⅝" (9cm)

Cut

12⅝" (32cm)

Join border fabrics to the right and left of the central area and sew them. The inner side seam allowance should be ⅜" (1cm). The outer side seam allowance should be ¾" (2cm).

③ ⅜" (1cm) seam allowance

11¾" (30cm)

15¾" (40cm)

3⅛" (8cm)

22" (56cm)

22" (56cm)

Cut

3⅝" (9cm)

Join border fabrics above and below the central area and sew them. The inner side seam allowance should be ⅜" (1cm). The outer side seam allowance should be ¾" (2cm).

Instructions

1) Take care of the appliqué, attach the border, and complete the top section.
2) Sandwich the cotton batting and the backing to the top, tack it, and start quilting.
3) Cut the cotton batting as shown in the diagrams. Fold the top back and wrap it up.
4) Fold the backing's seam allowance and blindstitch it to the folded-back top.
5) Create the petals and leaves and sew them on.

Instructions

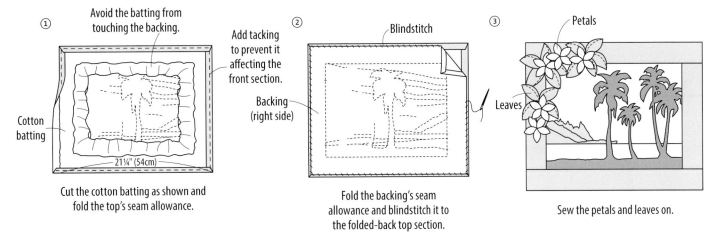

① Avoid the batting from touching the backing.

Add tacking to prevent it affecting the front section.

Cotton batting

21¼" (54cm)

Cut the cotton batting as shown and fold the top's seam allowance.

② Blindstitch

Backing (right side)

Fold the backing's seam allowance and blindstitch it to the folded-back top section.

③ Petals

Leaves

Sew the petals and leaves on.

How to Attach the Petals

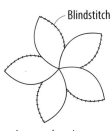

Blindstitch

Arrange them in a windmill shape and unite them at the center. Only blindstitch them on one side.

How to Attach the Leaves

Unite five leaves at the center, layer them on the main body, and sew them on by quilting the leaves' veins.

Photocopy at 100%

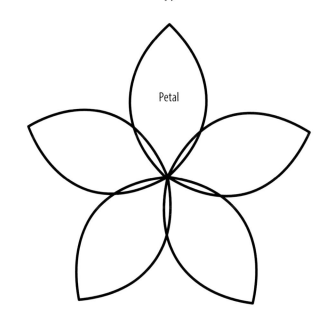

Petal

Materials

Appliqué fabric: fabric scraps (as needed)

Spadix appliqué fabric: 7⅞" x 4" (20 x 10cm)

Petals appliqué fabric (two types): 11¾" x 7⅞"
(30 x 20cm) each

Leaves appliqué fabric (two types): 15¾"x 11¾"
(40 x 30cm) each

Manta rays appliqué fabric (two types): 7⅞" x 5⅞"
(20 x 15cm) each

Border fabric: 17¾" x 19⅔" (45 x 50cm)

Cotton batting: 19⅔" x 19⅔" (50 x 50cm)

Backing fabric: 19⅔" x 19⅔" (50 x 50cm)

Thick fusible web: as needed

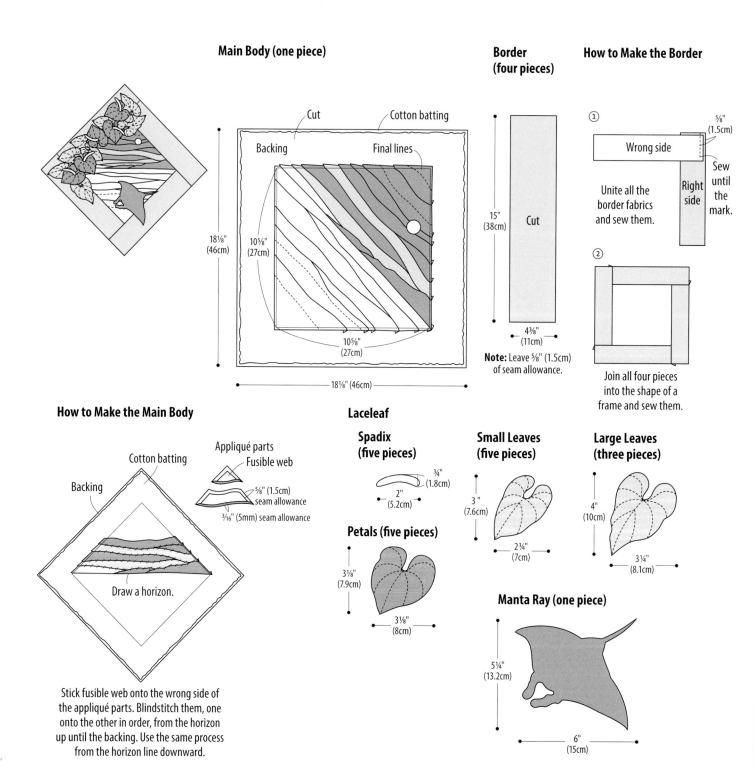

Main Body (one piece)

Cut
Cotton batting
Backing
Final lines

18⅛" (46cm)

10⅝" (27cm)

10⅝" (27cm)

18⅛" (46cm)

Border (four pieces)

Cut

15" (38cm)

4⅜" (11cm)

Note: Leave ⅝" (1.5cm) of seam allowance.

How to Make the Border

① Unite all the border fabrics and sew them.

Wrong side

Right side

⅝" (1.5cm)

Sew until the mark.

② Join all four pieces into the shape of a frame and sew them.

How to Make the Main Body

Cotton batting
Backing
Draw a horizon.

Appliqué parts
Fusible web
⅝" (1.5cm) seam allowance
3/16" (5mm) seam allowance

Stick fusible web onto the wrong side of the appliqué parts. Blindstitch them, one onto the other in order, from the horizon up until the backing. Use the same process from the horizon line downward.

Laceleaf

Spadix (five pieces)

¾" (1.8cm)

2" (5.2cm)

Petals (five pieces)

3⅛" (7.9cm)

3⅛" (8cm)

Small Leaves (five pieces)

3 " (7.6cm)

2¾" (7cm)

Large Leaves (three pieces)

4" (10cm)

3¼" (8.1cm)

Manta Ray (one piece)

5¼" (13.2cm)

6" (15cm)

Instructions

1) Sandwich the cotton batting and the backing. Take care of the appliqué and complete the central section.
2) Create the border. Layer it over the wrong side of the center created in step 1 and sew its edges.
3) Turn the border right side out, and blindstitch it to the central section.
4) Create the laceleaf and the manta ray. Sew them.

How to Make the Laceleaf & Manta Ray

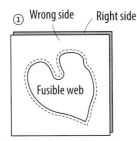

① Wrong side Right side

Fusible web

Stick a piece of fusible web, cut into the shape of the motif, onto one side of it. Join them together and sew the edges of the fusible web. For more detailed instructions, see pages 61 and 107.

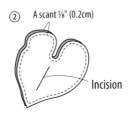

② A scant ⅛" (0.2cm)

Incision

Cut it out while leaving a scant ⅛" (2mm) seam allowance. Make an incision on the fusible web and on its opposite side. Turn right side out.

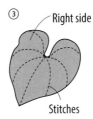

③ Right side

Stitches

Stitch the motif.

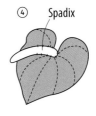

④ Spadix

Blindstitch the spadix to attach it to the petal.

Instructions

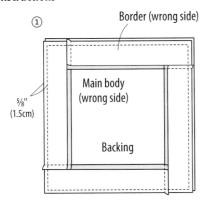

①

Border (wrong side)

Main body (wrong side)

Backing

⅝" (1.5cm)

Join the border with the main body's wrong side and sew all the edges.

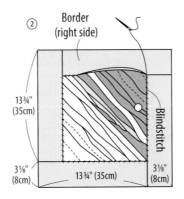

②

Border (right side)

Blindstitch

13¾" (35cm)

3⅛" (8cm)   13¾" (35cm)   3⅛" (8cm)

Turn the border right side out, and blindstitch it to the central area.

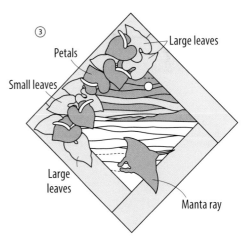

③

Petals   Large leaves

Small leaves

Large leaves

Manta ray

Attach the laceleaf and the manta ray by sewing them.

◼ Patterns

You can download the pattern files shown on pages 110–126 at foxpatterns.com/quiltingbold.

01

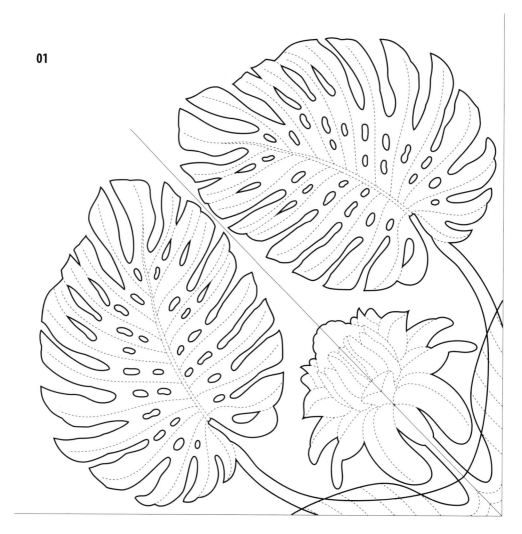

Photocopy at 400%

02

Photocopy at 280%

03

Photocopy at 400%

03

04

Photocopy at 200%

05

Photocopy at 400%

07

08

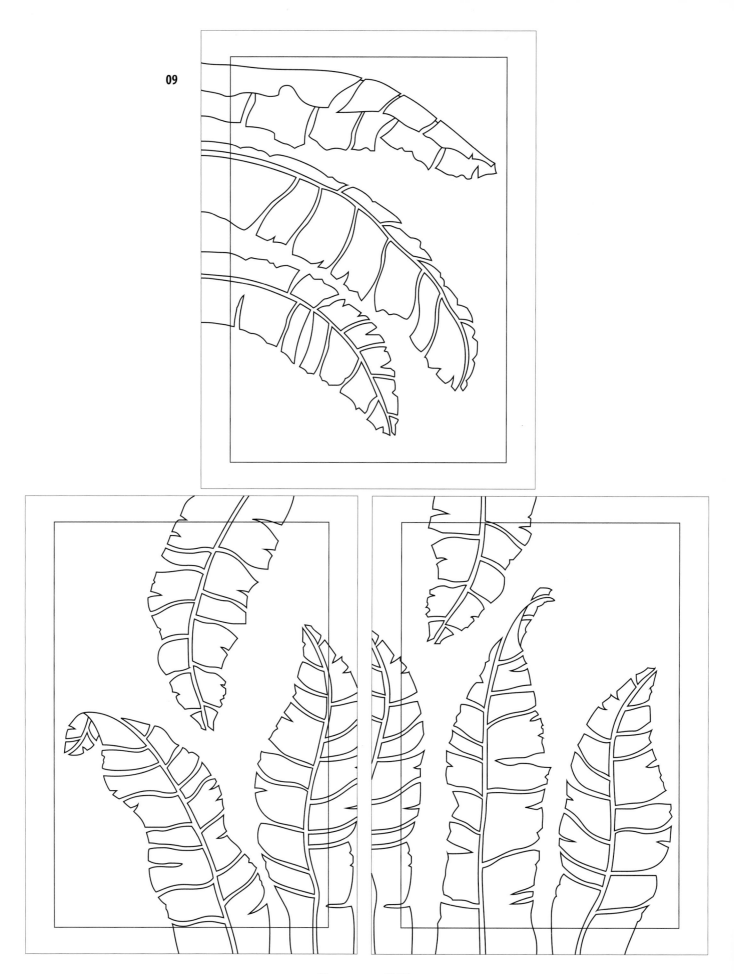

09

Photocopy at 400%

10

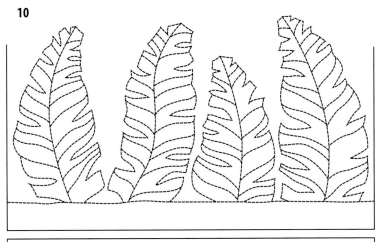

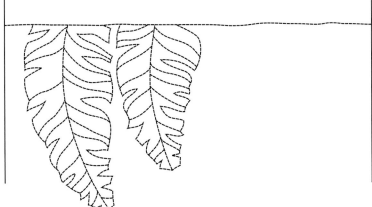

Photocopy at 400%

11

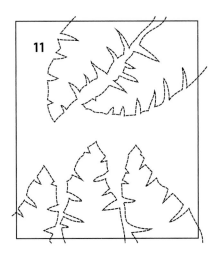

Photocopy at 400%

12

Photocopy at 500%

13

Photocopy at 800%

14

Photocopy at 750%

15

Photocopy at 600%

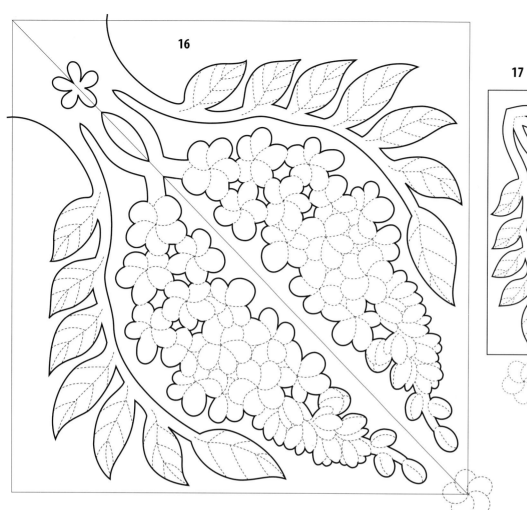

16

17

Photocopy at 400%

Photocopy at 400%

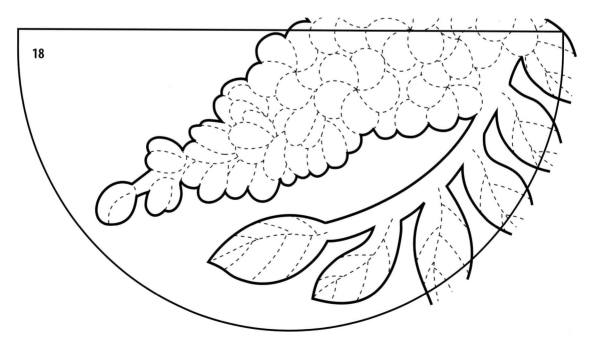

18

Photocopy at 400%

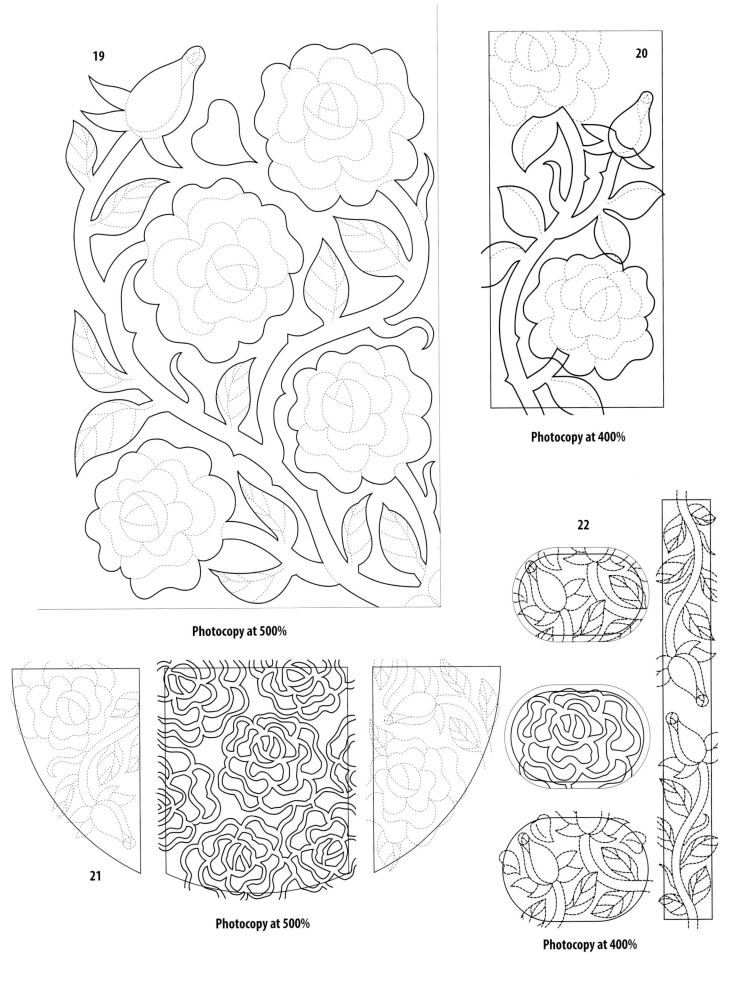

19

20

Photocopy at 400%

22

Photocopy at 500%

21

Photocopy at 500%

Photocopy at 400%

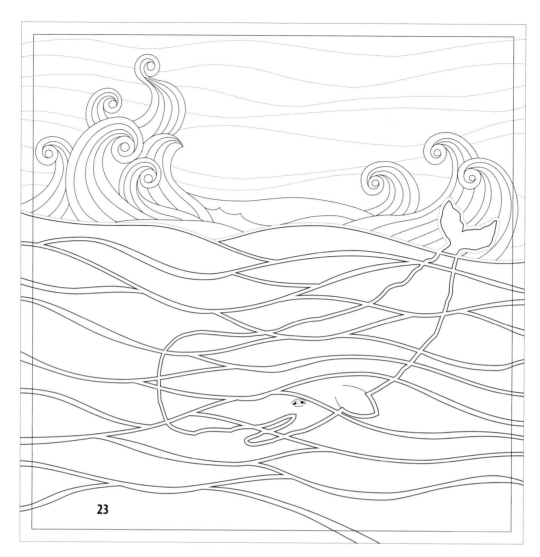

Photocopy at 800%

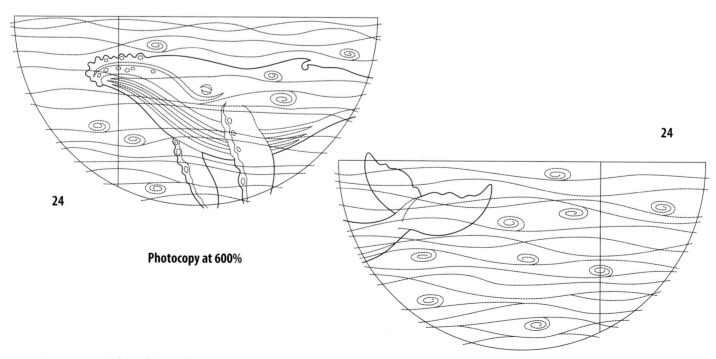

Photocopy at 600%

24

24

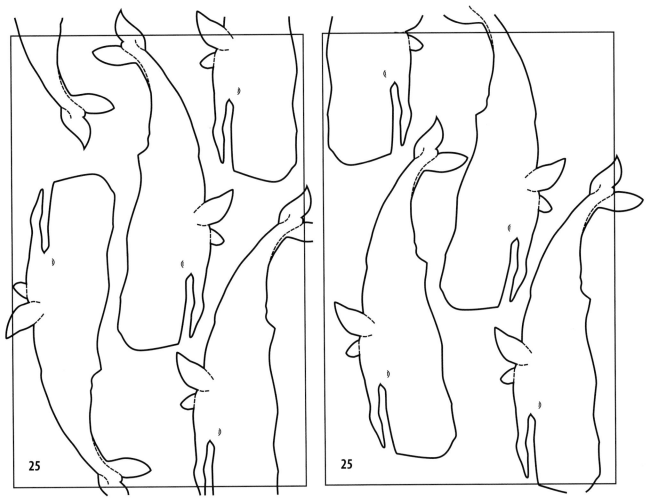

25 25

Photocopy at 300%

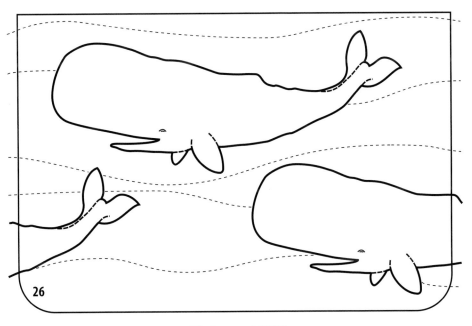

26

Photocopy at 250%

27

28

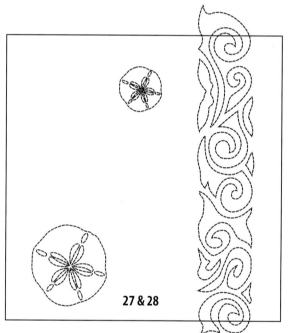

27 & 28

Photocopy at 400%

31

32

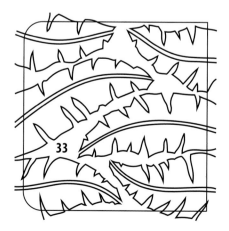

33

Photocopy at 400%

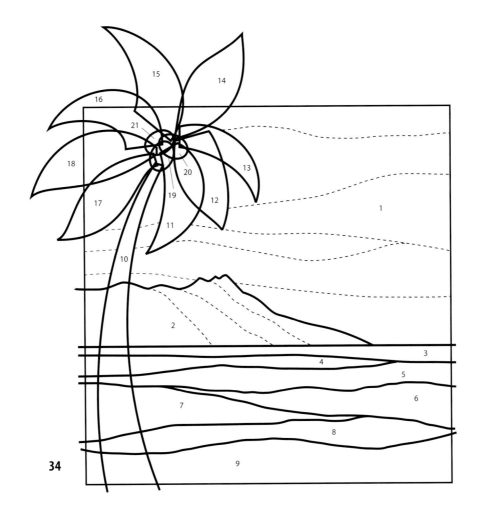

34

Photocopy at 250%

35

Photocopy at 400%

36

Photocopy at 225%

Afterword

Designing quilt patterns from zero might be hard, but taking existing patterns and developing a new design from them is surprisingly easy.

This book has explained how to make practical use of such designs, but I hope you can take these as guidance and make your own quilts. If you make a quilt that is different from the ones in this book, I'm convinced it'll convey its own spark of originality.

While I was preparing the quilts that are published here, my mother passed away. My memory of quilting at my mother's bed before she passed will remain with me.

I am so thankful for my mother, who always gave me so much. I'd like to dedicate this book to her.

Meg Maeda

About the Author

Meg Maeda

Meg Maeda is a graphic designer, quilt designer, author of quilting books, and public speaker on topics of quilting. She graduated from the graphic design department of Tama Art University. Her talent for design, which has underpinned her many years working as a graphic designer, has allowed her to manufacture fresh styles of quilt with highly original designs. Today, she continues her work as a graphic designer while teaching 15 classes a month, as well as giving seminars in quilting academies in the United States.

Her books include *Quilted Accessories in a Hawaiian Style, Quilts that Flower in Hawaii* (from Patchwork Tsuushinsha), *Hawaiian Designer Bags, Quilts that Inhabit Hawaii*, and *A Room with Hawaiian Quilts* (from Graphic-sha Publishing Co.)

Find more of her work on her website: heartandart.amebaownd.com

Index

Note: Page numbers in **bold** indicate project and patterns (in parentheses).